Tragic No More

TRAGIC NO MORE

*Mixed–Race Women
and the
Nexus of Sex and Celebrity*

Caroline A. Streeter

UNIVERSITY OF MASSACHUSETTS PRESS
Amherst and Boston

Copyright © 2012 by University of Massachusetts Press
All rights reserved
Printed in the United States of America

ISBN 978-1-55849-985-0 (paper); 984-3 (hardcover)

Designed by Sally Nichols
Set in Adobe Caslon Pro
Printed and bound by Thomson-Shore, Inc.

Library of Congress Cataloging-in-Publication Data

Streeter, Caroline A., 1962–
Tragic no more : mixed-race women and the nexus of sex and
celebrity / Caroline A. Streeter.
p. cm.
Includes bibliographical references and index.
ISBN 978-1-55849-985-0 (pbk. : alk. paper) — ISBN 978-1-55849-984-3 (hardbound : alk.
paper) 1. American literature—21st century—History and criticism. 2. Race in literature.
3. Racially mixed women in literature. 4. Racially mixed people in motion pictures.
5. Racially mixed women—Race identity—United States. I. Title.
PS231.R32S77 2012
810.9'3522—dc23

2012031201

British Library Cataloguing-in-Publication Data
A catalogue record for this book is available from the British Library.

To my family:
James, Lou, and Vicky Streeter

CONTENTS

ACKNOWLEDGMENTS

I would like to thank my colleagues in UCLA's Department of English and the Ralph J. Bunche Center for African American Studies. I am especially grateful to Richard Yarborough, Kathleen McHugh, and Harryette Mullen for insightful readings of the manuscript in its early stages, and to Arthur Little and King-kok Cheung for unflagging support throughout the process. For invaluable research assistance, I thank Courtney Johnson, Tara Lake, Brandy Underwood, and Kimberly McNair.

I remain inspired by the memory of Barbara Christian, who took me under her wing when I was in the graduate program in Ethnic Studies at UC Berkeley. Among the many brilliant professors I worked with at Berkeley, I especially thank Trinh T. Minh-ha for all I learned while studying with her. For the friendship and intellectual camaraderie at Berkeley that helped get my fledgling ideas about mixed race and popular culture off the ground, thank you to Kimberly McClain DaCosta, Rebecca King O'Ríain, Cynthia Nakashima, Kaaryn Gustafson, and Kendra R. Wallace.

I am grateful to Herman Gray and to Angela Davis for their inestimable guidance in making the transition from dissertation to book, and to the Center for Cultural Studies at UC Santa Cruz for providing the opportunity to work with them.

Thanks to the many friends and colleagues who offered opportunities to share this work as it took shape, among them: Toni Irving, Dwight

McBride, Arlene Keizer, Hiram Pérez, Maria P. P. Root, Alex Lubin, Herman DeBose, Loretta Winters, and Ifeoma Nwangkwo, and to Judy Godfrey, Kathryn Best Siefker, and the Grace Museum in Abilene, Texas. Thank you to Michele Elam for being a generous mentor and reader.

Kathryn Talalay was exceptionally gracious in sharing her encyclopedic knowledge of Philippa Schuyler's life with me. Her biography stands as the definitive work on Schuyler. I thank her for an interview that proved pivotal in my analysis of Schuyler in relation to contemporary figures such as Halle Berry.

I wrote this book in the company of others. I extend deep thanks to all of my writing partners over the years, especially Asali Solomon, Antoinette Chevalier, Maylei Blackwell, Yogita Goyal, Sarita See, and Linda Kim.

Many thanks go to Bruce Wilcox and Carol Betsch at the University of Massachusetts Press, and to the book's copy editor, Katherine D. Scheuer, for their remarkable patience.

I could not have written this book without the unconditional love of my parents, my sister, and my friends. For encouragement and support, I thank my dear friend Ed Cohen, who has seen me through all the stages of getting this book done. For deep and abiding friendship, I thank Lisa Ginsburg, Erin Kelly, Christina Ravelo, Anne Semans, Linda Nash, Jim Hanford, Bill Harrison, Maisha T. Winn, Jocelyn Miller, and Libby Lewis. And for the privilege of being in their lives as they grow, I thank Roxy and Lily Semans, Ezequiel, Michaela, and Gina Gwiazda, Helen and Peter Nash, Benjamin and Sara Ginsburg-Ball, and Iman and Rayha McPherson.

Chapter 4 is a revised and expanded version of "Faking the Funk? Mariah Carey, Alicia Keys, and (Hybrid) Black Celebrity," in *Black Cultural Traffic: Crossroads in Global Performance and Popular Culture,* edited by Harry J. Elam Jr. and Kennell Jackson (Ann Arbor: University of Michigan Press, 2005), 185–207, and is reprinted here by permisson.

Tragic No More

Introduction

The year 2008's historic spectacle of an African American man and a white woman running for President illuminates the ways in which the nation still contends with the difficult, unfinished business of a society configured through structural inequalities of race and gender. During the protracted primary campaigns of Barack Obama and Hillary Rodham Clinton, many aspects of public discourse became consumed by the troubling history of white-black interracial sexuality and the charged politics of black/white mixed-race identity.

Tragic No More takes up the compulsive attention to racial boundaries in the United States and explores why female figures are so often the visual representation of race mixing. This book is a multidisciplinary study of women on the color line—black/white women and their role in the simultaneous creation and undoing of racial categories. I analyze black/white femininity through fictional characters in selected novels and television, as well as through examples of biracial women in music and film who achieved celebrity status in the 1990s and after. I have also included selected narratives of black/white women from earlier decades that became re-contextualized in the late twentieth century. My work joins a significant body of texts published since the first decade of the new millennium, which are in dialogue across a range of topics that engage mixed race in the United States. This critical mass of exceptional work constitutes an emerging academic field of cultural studies in mixed race. The field is radically multidisciplinary, including historiographies of inter-racial romance and marriage,[1] research about contemporary biracial iden-tity[2] and the multiracial movement,[3] and critical theory in the humanities engaging literature, film, and performance.[4]

In this book I argue that women of black and white descent act as light-ning rods illuminating how the historical trauma of race relations plays out in current social life. Black/white women exercise this powerful triggering function because they resonate with the historical mulatto of American culture. Whereas contemporary mixed race is undeniably "tragic no more," the tragic mulatto has not been displaced. This is because contemporary figures of mixed race trigger the mulatto of historical memory. Mixed-race people may be our future, but at the present time they also function as vectors for uncanny returns to the past. My study of black/white women theorizes their significance as markers of sameness and difference on the boundary between the races, and on the spectrum of femininity among representations of African American women. The deeply troubled history of interracial sexuality is a critical part of what makes mixed-race people a repressed yet crucial aspect of America's national identity. As both the products of miscegenation and potential agents of interracial sex, black/white women symbolize a constitutive knot of dread and desire.

In the pages that follow, I identify two frameworks for understanding mixed race in the United States today. One is historical, derived from the abject condition of slaves and shaped by asymmetrical power relations. It remains a powerful narrative in African American communities. The other framework is more recent, oriented toward capturing the significance of contemporary social change since the 1990s. What the two frameworks share is engagement with the fraught terrain of interracial sexuality and the conundrum of racially hybrid identities. The conjunction of these narratives facilitates, on one hand, a reinscription of the so-called tragic mulatto as emblematic of the troubled past. At the same time, contempo-rary discourse invokes the tragic mulatto precisely to refute any lingering stigma attached to late twentieth-century mixed-race identity.

To declare mixed race is "tragic no more" is a virtual truism, as ample evidence indicates its apparent incorporation as a valid American identity, along with the integration of interracial couples and multiracial families in the general social landscape.[5] The nation's first generation of so-called post-Loving[6] children are nearing forty, and they are a dizzyingly diverse group, reflecting the growth of Latino and Asian populations and embodying the inevitable "exotic" mixtures of a global society. Mixed-race people are indeed attractive representations of multicultural diversity and seem to gesture toward the eventual diffusion of racial conflict. Healthy biracial identities and widely admired mixed-race icons seem to repudiate the tragic mulatto stereotype.

In 1993 *Time* magazine published a special issue called "The New Face of America: How Immigrants Are Shaping the World's First Multicultural Society."[7] The cover—a woman's face—was a high-tech amalgamation "created by a computer from a mix of several races." *Time* baptized her the new Eve. The issue contained essays charting the histories and present statuses of different population groups in the United States. One noted a sense of comfort and familiarity with the narratives of Europeans and the well-known foundational metaphor of our nation as a melting pot. Still, *Time* resisted a rosy image of history, noting the phobic responses to undesirable difference such as the imperative for nineteenth-century immigrants to anglicize their names and the various quotas imposed by immigration acts of the 1920s.[8] Acknowledging that the metaphor of the melting pot did not capture the United States of the late twentieth century, as the issue reached the contemporaneous period, *Time* transitioned to the term "multicultural."

Although *Time* did not shrink from shameful chapters of American history related to racism—slavery, genocide, forced relocations, segregation—one could sense the easing of tension as the issue wound down to essays about interracial marriages, mixed-race children, and multiracial families. The trajectory was linear yet also strangely circular—from amalgamated Eve to real-life race mixing.

The ambivalent status of race in "The New Face of America" betrays deep anxieties that are central to this book. America's late twentieth-century manifestation of mixed race does not signal an endpoint to racial categorization. It is, rather, evidence of the ways race morphs to accommodate new historical conditions. Whereas *Time*'s new Eve demonstrates the ways technology can be used to manage apprehension about race, similar technologies unearth traumatic historical conditions. A striking example is 1998's revelation that Thomas Jefferson fathered children with his slave Sally Hemings.[9]

These contradictions are evidence that the mulatto figure has not been displaced. Rather, the contemporary black/white woman's charged status derives from the persistent ways the mulatto ruptures linear time. The unmasking of the late Senator Strom Thurmond by Essie Mae Washington-Williams is a case in point. When the public learns that Thurmond actively disowned his biracial daughter, perpetuating the secrecy and disavowal analogous to those of a nineteenth-century slave owner, Americans are plunged into a time warp. In 2003 we experienced an uncanny return to 1803—to Thomas Jefferson and Sally Hemings. The mulatto figure is critical to this phenomenon of reinscription and return.

My analysis owes much to the work of feminist critics who have studied the mulatto figure in literature and film. These scholars theorize the question of why this narrative figure is so often female—is, in other words, a mulatta.[10] Feminist critics have revisited the tragic mulatto character by mining slave narratives,[11] novels and popular culture,[12] visual art,[13] and cinema.[14] These studies offer provocative readings of topics such as the passing narrative, mulattas as idealized images of black female beauty, and the tragic mulatto of narrative melodrama. Feminist scholarship focuses on mulatta women to parse relationships between literary narrative and social history, including how gender ambiguity sheds new light on passing narratives.[15] Literary[16] and film[17] studies also propose ways in which homoerotic desire complicates the heterosexual imperative[18]—a provocative reading given other interpretations of the mulatta as proxy for a white woman, and as such a repudiation of black women's femininity.[19] My study of gender and mixed race in 1990s literary, visual, and celebrity culture is closely engaged with feminist scholarship theorizing the mulatta's role as a narrative figure of mediation,[20] and her unique status as a visual signifier.[21]

The black/white woman is a critical symbol of racial passing and a key figure in the fraught politics of skin color, which has particularly charged ramifications for black women.[22] In the chapters that follow, I foreground the sexual and visual dynamics of the black/white woman's mediating role, exploring the signifying function of sexuality and the visual among African Americans. Feminist scholars have written at length about the mulatta's important mediating role in the oppositional model characterizing white versus black female sexuality. A notorious Brazilian adage neatly summarizes the way cultural stereotypes reveal articulations of race and gender. Declaring "white women are for marrying, mulattas for

fornication and black women for service,"[23] the colloquialism underscores
the feminist analysis of gender as a contingent historical formation, and
as such not a natural quality consistently attributed to all female bodies.[24]
Literary depictions of gender in American slavery pinpoint the mulatta's
illumination of the sexual resonance inherent in racial binaries. Namely,
the mulatta in slavery, or under slave-like conditions, mediates the space
between white women's virtuous asexuality and black women's uninhibited (bestial) sexual appetites.

Although late twentieth-century popular culture representations of
black/white women are related to historical images of the literary and cinematic mulatto, they depart radically from those textual iterations in the
way that interracial sexuality is depicted. Interracial marriage is relevant
to my analyses because the parents' relationship influences the ways black/
white women are represented. Since the 1990s sexuality has often been
exploited to trigger provocative images of miscegenation.

The black/white woman is a key figure in what I call the new marketing of miscegenation, where visual representation is a driving factor. In
a cultural environment of transformed sexual mores—from the emergence of the birth control pill to billboards urging people to get tested
for AIDS—black/white women's mediating function can be unambiguously and explicitly sexual. However, mixed-race scholarship has been
slow to reconcile a strong impulse in the field, namely, emphasizing the
normalization of mixed race through a focus on interracial marriage and
healthy biracial identities, at the expense of deeper analysis of the ways
contemporary culture draws on the traumatic historical archive of interracial sexuality.

The gender and race formation of the interracial couple fundamentally
shapes the cultural work black/white women perform on the boundary.
The Civil Rights era is bracketed by two singular events, which together
symbolize extreme ends of the representational spectrum of the interracial
relationship in the United States. In 1955, fourteen-year-old Emmett Till,
a boy from Chicago visiting his family in Mississippi, was brutally beaten
and lynched for "whistling at a white woman." Till's murder demonstrated
the easy entitlement white Southerners could exercise as a function of race
privilege. The violence of lynching had long been rationalized through
the myth that white men were honor-bound to protect vulnerable white
woman from rape by black men. This conflation of racial terrorism and

gender dominance—namely, white's men's patriarchal prerogative to discipline and punish black male and white female sexuality—was reinforced at the levels of law enforcement and the courts.

Emmett Till's lynching became a turning point in the battle for Civil Rights due to Mamie Till Mobley's decision to display her son's body in an open casket. Widely circulated photographs of the horribly mutilated boy literally gave a face to the depraved, patently evil extent to which white racism could go. The spectacular nature of Till's lynching, a shocking wake-up call for Americans unfamiliar with the deeply embedded sexual violence endemic to southern racism, made his murder a galvanizing event.

The second definitive bracketing moment marking the opposite end of the representational spectrum of interracial sexuality occurred in 1967, when the United States Supreme Court invalidated the nation's remaining miscegenation laws in the decision *Loving v. Virginia*.[25] The plaintiff couple, Richard Loving (white) and Mildred Jeter (black/Native American), lived in the same county and went to high school together. In 1958, shortly after they were married in Washington, D.C., the Lovings returned to Virginia where they were arrested and subsequently charged with violating the state's ban on interracial marriage. In January 1959, the couple pleaded guilty and were sentenced to one year in jail. However, the court suspended their sentences provided they would leave the state and not return together for twenty-five years. They resided in Washington, D.C., until they won their appeal.

The Supreme Court identified the doctrine of white supremacy as the subtext of miscegenation law, and as such a violation of the right to equal protection. However, the right to privacy was invoked as the most important determining factor in overturning miscegenation laws. And in asserting a white *man's* right to privacy, the Court decision was, symbolically at least, of a piece with white men's historical sexual prerogatives. Cultural images casting white women as sexually vulnerable to black men begs the question of how likely the Supreme Court would have been to revise laws prohibiting interracial marriage had the test case been composed of a black man and a white woman. The casting of interracial marriage as the right to privacy feeds the image of romantic love so prevalent in cultural narratives of interracial relationships. However, this idealistic notion fails to account for at least two things; first, the rarity of marriages between black women and white men, and second, the persistent exploitation of images of interracial sex—the marketing of miscegenation.

In 2007, the fortieth anniversary of *Loving* was celebrated in mainstream media and the scholarly world. The presence of Mildred Loving underscored how recently it had been decided and, with her subsequent death in 2008, added a retrospectively poignant note. The symbolic focus on this case in academe and cultural representation does not reflect the dominant parameters of interracial marriage in the United States. Studies of mixed race emphasize the rapid rise in interracial marriage rates since *Loving*. However, these unions occur against the backdrop of an over-whelming norm: marriage as a practice between people of the *same* race. Not only does white-black intermarriage remain rare in this country, where it comprises "only 0.6% of total marriages in the U.S. today";[26] these unions remain less common than any other form of interracial marriage, in 2010 accounting for 11.9 percent of the total.[27]

Emmett Till's fate is belied by post-*Loving* statistics showing that the majority of white-black marriages take place between white women and black men. Such unions outnumber by at least two to one marriages between black women and white men.[28]

Theories considering the social and economic contours accounting for interracial marriage rates coexist with a charged conversation about how the gendered difference in white-black intermarriage is grounded in the sexual fallout of slavery. In *Black Macho and the Myth of the Superwoman* (1978), Michele Wallace argues that black men's sexual desire for white women is an indication of these men's failure to fulfill the revolutionary potential of the Black Power movement, settling instead for possession of the white female body denied to them during slavery.[29] Although not all scholars agree with Wallace's provocative assessment of the gendered politics of Black Power, her critique of how slave-era images—hypersexual black men and masculine black women—play out in social life is echoed by contemporary black feminists.

A decade later in *Mixed Blood: Intermarriage and Ethnic Identity in Twentieth-Century America,* Paul R. Spickard also attributes the gendered pattern in white-black intermarriage to the mutually held sexual stereotypes of history. In addition, he cites contemporary factors: "ethnic chic—white interest in the lives of black people" and "a loosening of sexual mores that made white women suddenly available to black men."[30]

Indeed, myths attributing sexual qualities to gender and race are potent cultural scripts with real effects, and in many ways more accessible than somewhat dry models that portray interracial marriage as a function of the rapprochement of social classes.

For this reason, it is helpful to examine mixed-race literature produced in the 1990s, especially in the memoir genre, as a way of fleshing out historical conditions and contexts that made marriage between white women and black men a more likely prospect than in earlier decades. For example white women's greater autonomy, access to resources, and ability to live independently in the urban metropolis gave them more opportunities to meet and develop relationships with black men of similar educational background and shared interests. To consider the impact of *Loving* beyond the discursive parameters of private life is to acknowledge how interracial marriage fundamentally destabilizes the social order.

The ubiquity of the *Loving* case as the citational touchstone for mixed-race studies narrows the critical lens scholars use to theorize interracial relationships.[31] Alex Lubin points to the example of LeRoi and Hettie Jones as better symbolizing the social and political factors at play in interracial unions of the post–Civil Rights era. The 1958 marriage between Jones, seminal poet of the Black Arts Movement (now known as Amiri Baraka), and Hettie Cohen, of white and Jewish descent, was emblematic of interracial unions formed against the backdrop of bohemian New York— especially Greenwich Village—a cultural scene peopled with diverse artists, writers, and intellectuals.[32]

During the so-called Freedom Summer of 1964, the voter registration drive organized by the Congress on Racial Equality (CORE) brought many young white people from throughout the United States to the South. This setting facilitated interracial encounters between like-minded adults such as African American writer Alice Walker and white Jewish lawyer Mel Leventhal, who met through Civil Rights activism and were the first interracial couple married in Mississippi.[33]

Crucially, then, interracial sexuality and interracial marriage are not the same. This disparity between reality and cultural images points to the necessity of considering interracial sexuality and marriage as a politics of representation.

Media representations of the 1990s, continuing into the new millennium, graphically exploit the hyper-feminine white woman and oversexed black man of racial stereotype. This shameless flaunting of taboo—the new marketing of miscegenation—is especially evident in visual culture. The celebration of *Loving* jars with the continual production of images of interracial sexuality as imminent erotic combustion between black men and white women. Print media have continued to exploit this stereotype as recently as *Vogue* magazine's June 2008 cover image of African American basketball star LeBron James and Brazilian supermodel Gisele Bündchen. The photograph features James in black athletic wear leaning forward and yelling, one hand dribbling a basketball while his other arm encircles Bündchen's waist. She, clad in a clingy green silk dress, smiles radiantly but steps away from him, as indicated by the backward flow of her blonde-streaked mane of hair. The image, almost comically overdetermined by cinema's King Kong and Fay Wray, echoes the racial and sexual stereotypes underlying the lynching of Emmett Till, namely, interracial sexuality depicted as aggressive black masculinity and endangered white femininity. In this book I show how cultural anxieties about interracial sexuality are mapped onto the black/white woman's body.

In the first chapter I start with the layered media response to the revelation in 2003 that the late Senator Strom Thurmond had an illegitimate biracial daughter, Essie Mae Washington-Williams. Washington-Williams's announcement of her paternity occurred just five years after science confirmed that Thomas Jefferson fathered children with Sally Hemings. Thurmond's deeply unethical and hypocritical sense of entitlement in confining Washington-Williams to a dark recess of the private sphere is a reminder of how firmly ensconced the nation's racial hierarchy remains. The strategies Washington-Williams used to reclaim agency offer compelling evidence of the seismic potential of mixed-race identity to shift the silencing, repressive, and destructive deployment of race in social life.

In chapter 2 I turn to Dorothy West's novel *The Wedding* (1995), its television adaptation (1998), and the media's contextualization of the broadcast. West's protagonist in this novel set in the 1950s, a blonde and blue-eyed African American woman whom many read as "white," became in the miniseries light-skinned, yet identifiably "black." Over the two-night broadcast of *The Wedding*, the news media contextualized this representation of interracial marriage on television by bracketing it with contemporary stories of interracial marriages and mixed-race people.

Although people of color are marginal in prime-time television, African American viewership constitutes a target market. In the case of *The Wedding*, black cultural politics influenced representations of mixed-race and black/white figures.

In chapter 3 I explore sex and femininity in Danzy Senna's novels. *Caucasia* (1996) is one of the first contemporary works of fiction depicting mixed-race identities in the post-*Loving* era. It illuminates the ways interracial marriage triggered different kinds of anxieties in the 1970s, when black identities become rearticulated through Afro-centric values reframing African American perspectives on interracial sexuality. The novel stages the deep tension between the image of the biracial child as a sign of hope—or even political resistance—and a more ominous perception of interracial relationships as, at best, assimilation on the part of blacks and, at worst, a practice of race traitors. I develop an analysis of racialized rites of girlhood—namely, how girls learn to be feminine in ways related to the cultural aspects of race or ethnicity.

My reading of Senna's *Symptomatic* considers her critique of the multi-racial movement in her portrayal of alienated biracial heroines of the early 1990s. The novel's representation of contemporary mixed race embodies many concerns expressed by black-identified biracial Americans wary of celebratory discourses of hybridity. Black/white women in *Symptomatic* move across and within racial boundaries as a function of the color of heterosexuality. The novel's bleak psychological landscape mourns the dying out of "real" racial and cultural identity.

Chapter 4 examines two award-winning iconic superstars, Mariah Carey and Alicia Keys, as examples of the complex dynamics at play in the marketing of black/white celebrity in the 1990s and the new millennium. Representations of Carey and Keys demonstrate two possible outcomes for the black/white woman in popular culture. Carey is an object lesson of how mixed race as a site of ambiguous identity triggers ambivalent responses. The evidence lies in how media continually frame Carey with subtle and explicit references to the tragic mulatto. I build a case for Keys as an example of how a black/white figure successfully finds the delicate balance between the privilege of mixed race and the imperative for artists in "black" genres to reflect black racial authenticity. The ten-year period between the release of Carey's first album in 1991 and that of Keys in 2001 corresponds with the establishment of mixed race as a discourse relevant in academia, social life, and politics, and intelligible to a wider American public through the medium of popular culture. Carey and Keys, who are both biracial and of racially "ambiguous" appearance—i.e., they have light skin and so-called Caucasian features—are nonetheless racialized differently. Representations of Carey crystallize the ways in which key aspects of the African American historical experience of mixed race, such as the one-drop rule, racial passing, and the perception of mixed identities as disavowals of blackness, return in the 1990s under deeply ambivalent circumstances.

In chapter 5 I argue that the relationship between the actresses Dorothy Dandridge and Halle Berry is a popular cultural inscription of the American mulatto's trajectory from tragedy to triumph. Berry's explicit invocation of Dandridge to contextualize her own achievement as the first African American—indeed as the first woman of color—to win a Best Actress Academy Award created the space for that narrative to be compelling in the new millennium. The notion of Berry being Dandridge's artistic heir, and fulfilling the latter's thwarted potential, became naturalized in media discourse and is likely to persist as a feature of Hollywood film history. This narrative arc becomes intelligible precisely because Dandridge and Berry are ideal symbols of how mixed race transitions from the past to the present. But in my analysis, past and present iterations of mixed race do not follow a linear path of progress. The mixed-race subject of the 1990s does not displace the mulatto. The family heritage that makes Dandridge "black"—having two African American parents—and Berry "biracial"—having one white and one black parent—does not substantially change their signifying function as sexual and visual mediators of the space between white and black femininity and on the spectrum of black women's femininity.

In the last chapter I analyze popular media representations of Philippa Schuyler (1931–1967), biracial daughter of the prominent African American writer George Schuyler and his white wife, Josephine Cogdell. As an internationally renowned concert pianist, Philippa Schuyler was a uniquely glamorous woman considered both a role model for African Americans and an exemplary bridge between the races. Whereas her father has remained a well-known figure among scholars, Schuyler's prominence during her lifetime contrasts dramatically with her virtual obscurity today. I examine selections from the exhaustive archive documenting her life and concert career in mainstream (white) American and

African American newspapers and magazines to read the politics of representation deployed by a racially bifurcated media to represent a black/white celebrity. Hailed as a prodigy and child genius, Schuyler became a media star at age three. She was identified as a "Negro" by the prevailing one-drop rule, and being the gifted daughter of a high-profile interracial couple made her biracial heritage all the more noteworthy. Media discourse clearly positioned Philippa as both an exemplary Negro and an exotic hybrid, making her, like the contemporary figures in my study, simultaneously African American and mixed race.

Philippa Schuyler seemed poised to make a historic breakthrough in the racially hermetic world of classical music, but ultimately American racism prevented her from pursuing a career in the United States. Although her death in 1967 was reported on the front page of the *New York Times* and noted in media throughout the world, Schuyler soon faded from cultural memory. Kathryn Talalay's definitive biography of the artist reintroduced Schuyler to the public in 1995, an ideal time for mixed-race discourse to narrate her life anew. Talalay's book unearthed her as an overlooked African American artist whose biracial identity was, in her own lifetime, relevant to popular cultural representation.

A decade ago Halle Berry purchased the film rights to Talalay's biography to produce a narrative film starring Alicia Keys as Philippa Schuyler. Berry's ambition to bring Schuyler's story to Hollywood, with Keys infusing the character with black/white authenticity, resembles the trajectory from Dandridge to Berry, using one black/white woman's triumph to rehabilitate another's tragic fate. The resurrection of Philippa Schuyler inscribes an arc from tragedy to triumph—a trajectory recurring repeatedly with black/white figures in the new millennium.

CHAPTER 1

Essie Mae Washington-Williams's Secrets and Strom Thurmond's Lies

Reclaiming that from which one has been disinherited is a good thing.
Self-possession in the full sense of that expression is the companion to self-knowledge.
Yet claiming for myself a heritage the weft of whose genesis is my own
disinheritance is a profoundly troubling paradox.

PATRICIA J. WILLIAMS

As the illegitimate daughter of late South Carolina senator Strom Thurmond, Essie Mae Washington-Williams has the proto-slavery mulatto/a experience of being the unacknowledged child of a white man from a powerful southern family and a young black woman working as a domestic servant in his household. Washington-Williams and a person such as President Obama represent, as individuals, the historical continuum of mixed race in the twentieth-century United States. This trajectory begins in the secrecy and disavowal of the slave era. President Obama is an example of black/white mixed race in the first post-*Loving* generation, leaping conventional boundaries and forging connections across profound distance and difference. However, Washington-Williams—the symbolic historical mulatto—inhabits the present, not the past. This rupture of linear time is the hallmark of what the black/white figure "does" in U.S. culture. The historical mulatto narrative and the mixed-race narrative of the late twentieth century have become like the double helix of DNA. They are mutually constitutive. Barack Obama's *Dreams from My Father* is one of the memoirs of the 1990s that paved the way for the public—even Washington-Williams herself—to grasp what it might mean to be both black and white.

As a young child, Essie Mae Washington-Williams was sent from her birthplace in South Carolina to Illinois. She grew up thinking her

parents were an aunt—her mother's sister—and an uncle. She met her
birth mother, Carrie Butler, when she was thirteen years old, and was
introduced to Strom Thurmond when she was sixteen. Upon Thurmond's
death in 2003, Washington-Williams came forward to make her status as
his daughter public.

The trope of black/white mixed race reflects the uneasy historical relationship between the state's punitive treatment of miscegenation and the
continual failure of laws and social proscriptions aimed at keeping people
of different races apart. In the gap between miscegenation law and the fact
of interracial relationships dwells an elaborate system of denial refined
over generations. Although Washington-Williams, born in 1925, is among
the oldest of biracial memoir authors, a number born in the 1950s shortly
before *Loving* relate similar family histories of abandonment by white
parents—including mothers. Examples of the latter include Gregory
Howard Williams's *Life on the Color Line: The True Story of a White Boy Who
Discovered He Was Black* (1995) and June Cross's *Secret Daughter: A Mixed
Race Daughter and the Mother Who Gave Her Away* (2006).[1]

As stringently as scholars have attempted in recent years to avoid dual-
isms in speaking of race, the term's meaning is not restricted to opposing
concepts. A dualism is also the state of having two parts. The so-called
mulatto/a is not only a creature of antagonistic concepts, but also a product of twin (and overlapping) narratives. Although dictionaries categorize
"mulatto" among dated terms, in the United States mulatto remains rec-
ognizable as descriptive of a dually constituted individual—born of one
black and one white parent—and a dually constituted group by virtue of
black and white ancestry.

Disavowal and disinheritance are the reciprocal constituents of the
peculiar state of limbo deriving from the logic of the one-drop rule. As
explained in the definitive study by F. James Davis, *Who Is Black?* (origi-
nally published in 1991)[2] this convention designates as black any person
with a traceable amount of black blood. According to that logic, one might
ask, "Who is *not* Black?" Indeed, the one-drop rule has functioned as the
crucial litmus test determining who is (or gets to be) white. Eva Saks explains that the statutes preventing interracial marriage were the lynchpin
in making "genealogy . . . the determinant of race, thereby marking former
slaves permanently as black and . . . as a genetic underclass." Miscegenation
law "stabilize[d] property in race by investing white blood with value and

arresting its circulation in the body politic. In so doing, miscegenation law constituted the human body as a property."[3] Racial classification in the United States is historically unstable. Standards of blood fractions determining race differed across the states—and could alter abruptly within a single state. For example, in 1910 the state of Virginia changed the fraction of blood determining blackness from one-fourth to one-eighth. Thus the one-drop rule worked to stabilize racial classification by establishing a consensus, one that was social, cultural, and, crucially, juridical, to make clear that one could not be white unless one was *not* black. Unlike the various statutes defining blood fractions, the one-drop rule was not formally codified in law. However, court rulings throughout the nation repeatedly confirmed the rule's implicit authority.[4]

As for African Americans' eventual adoption of the one-drop rule, Davis argues persuasively how powerfully racism alienates blacks from the white-dominated social world. Because anti-black racism extends to interracial relationships, families, and individuals, many bi- and multiracial African Americans—especially those who are visibly black—experience identity as *both* biracial *and* black. Studies of biracial identity and less formal publications relating personal and family experience, published over the period I focus on in this study (and continuing into our present twenty-one teens, if you will) attest to different racial public versus private identities. Many with black/white mixed-race heritage have a black public identity that coexists with one's private mixed-race experience.[5] The "new" phenomenon in contemporary mixed race is not the people themselves but the opening of a cultural space for posing challenging, discomfiting questions about race and nation.[6]

The state of hybridity—that is to say, mixture itself—is at the core of how black people became an intelligible group in the United States. The twisted logic of slavery mandated that Africans be rendered completely disoriented as to tribe and language. Over a period of two centuries, American-born slaves were repeatedly subjected to being robbed of their parents, children, and so on. The imperative to continually reconstitute a community with such a fragile hold on the conviction that one is, indeed, human demands profound improvisation. For the descendants of West African slaves, being at once fragmented and whole is the starting point for developing individual self-consciousness and the sense of being part of a particular group. Although relatively few bi- or multiracial blacks in

the United States are likely to "check more than one," mixed-race discourse draws its logic from black identity, a function of historical conditions that made so-called race mixture a norm.

Patricia Williams captures the work made imperative for the former
slaves to make the transition from being objects of property to becoming
subjects of history. W. E. B. Du Bois theorized the psychological outcome
of this historical trajectory as double consciousness.

> The Negro is a sort of seventh son, born with a veil,
> and gifted with second-sight in this American world,—
> a world which yields him no true self-consciousness,
> but only lets him see himself through the revelation of
> the other world. It is a peculiar sensation, this double-
> consciousness, this sense of always looking at one's self
> through the eyes of others, of measuring one's soul by
> the tape of a world that looks on in amused contempt
> and pity.[7]

The black/white individual inherits the imperative for related yet different psychological labor. And the weft, or particular weave of the mulatto narrative produces a striking temporal paradox. In the case of Essie
Mae Washington-Williams and Strom Thurmond, the story that unfurled
in 2003 showed how black/white mixed race produces historical disloca-
tions. In this case, breaks in the linear narrative of race relations played out
on the national stage of media, before the audience's very eyes.

When Washington-Williams made her identity public in 2003, she made
clear her objective was to be recognized as Thurmond's child. She said she
would not make a claim on Thurmond's estate. (Subsequently 2005's *Dear
Senator* indicates her vacillation in this regard.) Here the separation of syn-
onyms—heritage from inheritance—corresponds to what Patricia Williams
calls the dilemma of claiming "self-possession." For Washington-Williams
to aspire to self-possession as Thurmond's daughter, she must incorporate
two things. First, to be re-made as Thurmond's daughter is to accept her
origin, in the cradle of Strom Thurmond's disavowal of paternity, which
draws racial boundaries separating "blood family." Secondly, she must en-
dure disinheritance, the racial boundaries around his estate; an estate in-
debted to the labor extracted from her own maternal ancestors, both slave
and free.

Thurmond's extramarital relationship with Carrie Butler and the birth of Essie Mae were common knowledge in the small community of Edgefield, South Carolina—especially among the African Americans. The story was an ongoing subject of speculation outside the state, and even the topic of an investigative story published by the *Washington Post* in 1992.[8] As an architect of the so-called Dixiecrat rebellion against the increasingly progressive politics of the Democratic Party in the 1940s, Thurmond was instrumental in consolidating southern states' defiance of federally mandated civil rights legislation. Interestingly, Thurmond's 1948 run for the presidency ignited gossip about "the Governor's daughter," a fitting southern metaphor considering William Wells Brown's *Clotel; or, the President's Daughter: A Tale of the Southern States.*[9]

As the governor's and subsequently the senator's daughter, Washington-Williams represents the vexed nature of interracial relations in the South. Genteel southern culture makes the metaphorical concession that blacks are family so long as they remain social inferiors and any evidence of race mixing is repressed. As Washington-Williams relates, Thurmond spoke of his daughter in the third person, remarking to Carrie Butler upon first meeting Essie Mae, "You have a lovely young daughter" (36). In later years he expressed patriarchal magnanimity while withholding paternity: "You're a dear family friend from Edgefield . . . your family helped my family for a long time . . . we're really one family. Which is true, isn't it?" (116).

Thurmond's reputation as a dyed-in-the-wool white supremacist made him a notorious figure right up to his death. At a 2002 celebration of Thurmond's one-hundredth birthday, Mississippi senator Trent Lott's comments about his 1948 presidential campaign—"We're proud of it. And if the rest of the country had followed our lead, we wouldn't have had all these problems over all these years either"—caused such a furor that Lott was obliged to resign his own position as incoming Senate majority leader.[10] The instantaneous backlash from politicians such as Al Gore was an interesting sign of the turn in American culture against unrepentant nostalgia for the good old days of white supremacy, repudiating southern insistence on celebrating the Confederacy as cultural patrimony. Washington-Williams analogizes her position as the illegitimate daughter of a famous white supremacist to being "under a lifetime gag order" (160).

Washington-Williams faced an unenviable dilemma. Her search for wholeness involved the very real risk of even more loss. Given her tenuous

relationship with Thurmond, along with black Americans' justifiable out-
rage at his political stance, Washington-Williams performed her own
version of racial passing. Expressing the nuances of keeping her secret,
she articulates a long tradition among African Americans of protecting
those engaged in racial passing—in this case, both herself and Thurmond,
passing vis-à-vis his intimate relations with African Americans. Interracial sex alone taints the white race, amalgamating the blood passed down
from parent to child, circulating it "in the body politic" (Saks), and in so
doing demeaning its value. Washington-Williams summarizes the impact
of more than a half century wrestling with this conflicted legacy: "It's not
that Strom Thurmond ever swore me to secrecy. He never swore me to
anything. He trusted me, and I respected him, and we loved each other in
our deeply repressed ways, and that was our social contract" (190).

The ambivalence evident in these words was, for Washington-
Williams's carefully orchestrated "coming out" in late 2003, jettisoned in
favor of important discursive strains characterizing media representations
of mixed race in the new millennium. These are a careful civility and a
concerted effort to humanize white racism through the very interracial
relations revealing, in Thurmond's case, his engagement in interracial sexuality as politically, morally corrupt—a practice of gender and race entitlement. Southern gentility permeated the sequence of public disclosures.
The Thurmond family did not compel Washington-Williams to prove her
identity through DNA. Nor did they object to the South Carolina leg-
islature's vote to add Washington-Williams's name to a commemorative
Thurmond statue, showing more grace than Thomas Jefferson's "legitimate" descendants, who denied petitions from newly minted offspring to
become part of the Monticello association.[11]

As is now common knowledge, in 1998 DNA research confirmed that
Thomas Jefferson fathered children with his slave Sally Hemings. The evidence substantiated persistent, so-called rumors asserting that Jefferson
had a decades-long sexual relationship with Hemings. Before that time,
the story was habitually attributed to African American oral histories.
Jefferson historians disputed it well into the twentieth century.[12] Crucially, most of these experts dismissed archival evidence. During Jefferson's
second presidential campaign in 1802, several journals and newspapers
published "popular rhymes (and) songs . . . about Jefferson and Hemings."
Twentieth-century historians created the myth of "The Callendar Affair,"

calling the story an example of yellow journalism propagated by journalist James Thomas Callendar—admittedly Jefferson's sworn enemy.[13] However, historians also declined to give serious consideration to legitimate items of journalism. In 1873 an interview with Madison Hemings appeared in southern Ohio's *Pike County Republican.* Hemings convincingly described his childhood as Jefferson's child and slave. Several months later, the *Pike County Republican* published "the memoirs of Israel Jefferson, a former slave at Monticello who was friendly with Madison Hemings. Israel Jefferson corroborated Madison's claims to having been the President's child."[14]

The authority granted to genetic evidence is the result of scientific research that debunks the notion that people can be divided into races.[15] Although groups of people hailing from different parts of the globe share physical characteristics, the genetic deviations that produce these differences are vastly oversimplified. For example, melanin, the chemical responsible for skin color, can vary widely among people of the same race and between people of different racial groups. The ways human beings interpret difference is the powerfully determining factor in race relations. The weight given to genetic evidence in the Jefferson-Hemings example has disquieting overtones. On one hand technologies can refute the notion that there are essential blood differences between groups of human beings that are classified according to race. And, increasingly, these technologies serve the purpose of producing unimpeachable racial classification. In this case, the default to technology served to resolve a secret that for many would erode Jefferson's historical image. As we shall see, the narratives to recuperate the great man are quite similar to those used to rehabilitate Strom Thurmond.

The Thurmond family is to be commended for respecting Essie Mae Washington-Williams's claims without demanding DNA evidence. Still, their press statement, much as Thurmond did during his lifetime, kept Washington-Williams at a polite arm's length. The statement confirmed "Ms. Essie Mae Washington-Williams's claim to her heritage" and expressed the "hope this acknowledgement will bring closure for Ms. Williams."[16] Frank K. Wheaton, attorney and spokesperson for Washington-Williams, followed the unspoken rule that enable white families to honorably disavow members from the wrong racial side of the street. He underplayed Thurmond's abandonment of Washington-Williams by emphasizing the "mutual respect and appreciation" in their relationship.

Media representations took similar tones of civility and, above all, solicitousness toward Washington-Williams, framing her as living proof of Thurmond's deceit, but also of his all-too-human contradictions.[17] Washington-Williams's mother, however, was and remains oddly absent. On December 17, 2003, Frank K. Wheaton did not mention Carrie Butler in his prepared remarks at the South Carolina press conference introducing Washington-Williams to the world.[18] Nor did Dan Rather, later that same evening, refer to Carrie Butler by name, using instead the phrase "your mother."[19]

The conspicuous absence of Carrie Butler is especially odd given the legacy of absent white fathers and present black mothers in the construction of the mulatto/a. On *60 Minutes* (CBS), Dan Rather set the pattern virtually all journalists would follow. According to the transcript, Rather did not speak Carrie Butler's name. After noting her age and station in life (sometimes "domestic worker," often "maid") Rather shifted to the crux of the matter: how much was rape and how much was love? Gingerly, he posed the question made imperative by history: Was the relationship consensual? To which Washington-Williams gave the same modest reply she repeated in all her press interviews. Shyly admitting to knowing very little, having never asked, she suspects there was genuine affection between the two. Each time a comparable exchange took place one sensed palpable relief. In that pause, the very void we might imagine Carrie Butler to inhabit evaporates. And so although Strom Thurmond, staunch white supremacist, fathered a biracial child, the media helpfully clarify that he was *not* a rapist. This became the most important thing to know about Carrie Butler.

One imagines that Washington-Williams far prefers to imagine the unspoken contract she shared with her father was based on some vestige of love for her mother, an interracial love that humanized Strom Thurmond. For as we learn, putting Carrie Butler's body under erasure is critical to softening his hypocrisy, maintaining the image of Thurmond as simply a creature of his time. The facts, as related in *Dear Senator*, are cold and unrelenting: An impoverished sixteen-year-old Carrie Butler sent the infant Essie Mae to Pennsylvania to be taken care of by her sister. Essie Mae was a teenager when she learned Butler was her mother, and sixteen when Butler introduced her to Thurmond. This event took place in Edgefield, South Carolina. Essie Mae's first visit to the South was marked by shock at her relatives' abject poverty and stunned disbelief at Jim Crow.

By 1948, Carrie Butler was destitute and fatally ill, eventually dying of renal failure at the age of thirty-eight (143). That same year a hale and hearty Thurmond made his Dixiecrat run for the Presidency, his twenty-two-year-old bride (a former aide) at his side. Although *Dear Senator* is frustratingly short on details about Butler and contains no photographs of her, the memoir is unambiguous about the harsh effects of race and gender inequity on Carrie Butler's short life.

In the recuperation of Strom Thurmond, Carrie Butler was rendered in the negative—embodied only through what Thurmond did *not* do. The phenomenon of litotes—the understatement that highlights the fact—continually vexed the very repetition of the story meant to humanize him. Despite Carrie Butler's imposed absence, the thing Thurmond did not do continually invoked racist sexual entitlement.

When Essie Mae Washington-Williams came forward she stepped into the void left by her mother. This move gave Thurmond's supporters the opportunity to substitute for the questionable image associated with Carrie Butler one of benevolent patriarch. Washington-Williams's own ambivalence fueled this project. Thurmond's political cronies were unanimous in their defense of Thurmond on the basis of his having given Washington-Williams occasional (and for her, unpredictable) "gifts" of money. Thurmond's so-called generosity had clearly not included Carrie Butler. Still, a combination of collegial support, along with *Dear Senator's* wistful attempts to read signs of affection in the limited, eventually annual encounters with Thurmond, helped to accelerate the story's inevitable move out of the media spotlight. In *Dear Senator*, Washington-Williams voices her resentment at being manipulated by Thurmond's largesse, at one point calling the financial gifts "hush money." To my knowledge she reserved this kind of spunk for her memoir. Washington-Williams did not argue with the narrative framing Thurmond's financial assistance as an acceptable concession to fatherhood.

By the time she made her presence known, Essie Mae Washington-Williams was in her late seventies, and as such not subject to being eroticized as a younger black/white woman could be. She did, however, symbolize a bridge between the races, achieving the unlikely feat of humanizing, rather than humiliating, a radically polarizing symbol of white supremacy. When one reads the conclusion of *Dear Senator*, it appears that Washington-Williams resolved the shame of her illegitimate birth. This is a powerful move for a person of her generation. Her own words indicate a sense of personal transformation from tragic mulatto/a to biracial subject. By the conclusion of her book, she articulates this newfound self-image: "I am every bit as white as I am black, and it is my full intention to drink the nectar of both goblets" (223). Washington-Williams shares her intention to apply for membership in the Daughters of the American Revolution and the United Daughters of the Confederacy; she is eligible to join both by virtue of her Thurmond bloodline.[20]

Is Washington-Williams among the last of her kind—that is to say, one of a dwindling number of biracial Americans with a virtually slave-era mulatto/a experience? In 2009 the long-running African American weekly *Jet* magazine reported that Prince Albert of Monaco acknowledged fathering his own illegitimate biracial child. Such revelations are likely to increase before they diminish. With her courageous revelation, Essie Mae Washington-Williams produces a powerful counter-discourse to the shame black Americans have had to shoulder with regard to the history of race mixing. She models an admirable fortitude to withstand the terrible tension of secrets, to willingly risk shame through disclosure, and to craft of denial and disinheritance a semblance of self-knowledge.

CHAPTER 2

The Wedding's Black/White Women
in Prime Time

Dorothy West's novel *The Wedding's* movement into television media represents shifts in post–Civil Rights era politics. The changes include the nature of "positive" racial imagery, the politics of identifying with an elite class, and the repression of themes threatening contemporary investments in "racial authenticity." The important differences between film adaptation and the literary text include how they work through themes of racial passing, intra-racial prejudice and the politics of racial visibility more generally. I analyze the book with the miniseries to build an argument about the politics of translation across fields and genres. What are the stakes of adapting a work of literature to commercial television?

In *The Wedding* as commercial television, there is a tension between the generation of "positive" images—as defined in the historical moment of the late 1990s—and racial ambiguity. Halle Berry is the black/white woman figure in whom this tension is, at least provisionally, resolved. Although racial alliances are based on more than skin color, the film cannot quite accommodate that, given the imperative of having identifiably "black/er" characters albeit embodying the light-skinned ideal, especially as regards women.

On February 22 and 23, 1998, the ABC network broadcast an Oprah Winfrey–produced miniseries adapted from West's novel, published in 1995.[1] *The Wedding* focuses on a group of African Americans who spend their summers in "the Oval," an exclusive "colored" vacation enclave in the segregated Martha's Vineyard of 1953.[2] It is significant the miniseries was broadcast during African American History Month and shortly after Valentine's Day, for the narrative is about an African American community rarely depicted on television, and revolves around a central plot concerning an "interracial" love story. Dynamics of race, color, and class are critical factors in narrative.[3] West's story of this privileged group of well-educated professionals emphasizes that they are segregated not only by prevailing social convention, but also by choice. They feel superior to African Americans of lower socioeconomic classes as well as to many "white" people.[4] Taking place over a 24-hour period, the story focuses upon the Coles family, the most successful in the community.

Although the miniseries preserves the main plot of the novel, its narrative emphasizes aspects of West's story corresponding to a distinctly post–Civil Rights era agenda with regard to media representations. Oprah Winfrey's introductory remarks to the first night of the two-part broadcast highlighted *The Wedding*'s portrayal of professional and genteel African Americans, images that explicitly depart from conventional television narratives depicting blacks in situation comedies or, in prime-time dramas, as members of the criminal urban underclass.[5] In this respect, the miniseries corresponds to the post–Civil Rights era investment in producing film and television that not only includes African Americans, but also challenges demeaning representations.

The notion of a black television audience positively identifying with the insular African American elite of mid-century represents a significant transition in the politics of representation. The critique of the black middle class which emerged in Black Power rhetoric of the late 1960s and early 1970s signaled a rupture between strategies of assimilation long associated with the black middle class and a radical rejection of that ideology in favor of direct confrontations with institutional racism. Although West had by then begun work on *The Wedding*, she instinctively sensed that the shift in attitudes might limit her reading audience. Interviewed in 1987, West confirmed as much:

> It was fear of such criticism that prevented me from continuing work on my novel *The Wedding* . . . (this time) coincided with the Black Revolution, when many Blacks

> believed that middle-class blacks were Uncle Toms . . .
> I thought it was a good book that should be read, and
> I felt that if it received a negative review, no one would
> read it . . . During that time white publishers were very
> intimidated by militant Blacks . . . It was then that the
> revolution was at its peak, and I cared very deeply about
> its goals, and, therefore, I couldn't go on writing the
> novel.[6]

What made the 1990s a more fortuitous period for the publication of *The Wedding* and a good time to broadcast the television adaptation? Images of middle-class blacks have shifted significantly in recent decades. Herman Gray notes that the 1980s phenomenon of *The Cosby Show* constituted a significant historical marker in American television, indicating a multiracial public would avidly consume a narrative about a successful black middle-class family. Rather than being stigmatized as "Uncle Toms," these television characters were positive role models.[7] Oprah Winfrey, who in the twenty-first century has become the first African American billionaire, is one of the most culturally influential women in the United States who, like the fictional Huxtables, appeals as much to white Americans as she does to black Americans. The emergence of widespread celebrity worship has enabled a figure like Winfrey (as well as the real Bill Cosby—a multi-millionaire in his own right) to remain relatively untouched by the kind of political critique of the black privileged class that discouraged West from seeking publication of her novel until the 1990s.

At the same time, neither the professional middle-class Huxtables of television or a self-made billionaire like Winfrey quite approximate the colored elite that is the subject of *The Wedding*. As West writes, the complicated mechanism by which hierarchical status is calibrated among the African Americans of the Oval, which draws upon factors that include skin color, family heritage, education, profession, and economic status is virtually impenetrable to outsiders. The ways in which the novel and the miniseries historicize the maternal and paternal branches of the Coles family clarify the calculus that determines elite membership is rife with contradictions. West's critique of these contradictions and the way she links them to the hypocrisies of dominant society made the novel a success with readers of the 1990s. Although the miniseries excises aspects of plot that make significant interventions in conventional representation, it faithfully reproduces the aspect of the novel linking intra-racial skin color prejudice with interracial intolerance.

Although light skin color is not the only factor (nor even a consistent one) distinguishing African Americans of the Oval, it is a familiar attribute among families of the elite "colored" enclaves of the urban North.[8] The Wedding foregrounds the practice of selective marriage to raise the likelihood of light-skinned children. In the novel, this practice has resulted in families like the Coles, all of whom are virtually white in appearance. Of course, the appearance of whiteness is a highly subjective and situated phenomenon. Although light-skinned African Americans might be able to racially pass among white Americans (and even African Americans) unfamiliar with African Americans that look like them, the Oval recognizes the members of their community; they have an intimate history with the oxymoron of colored people that look white. The Wedding interrogates the idea of racial passing through the protagonist Shelby, the younger of the two Coles daughters. Shelby, with her light skin, blue eyes, and blonde hair, closely resembles the white maternal great grandmother living with the family. Through writing about "white looking" African Americans, West foregrounds the question "What is the meaning of racial passing?" for a contemporary audience.

Early in the novel, Shelby's memory of a childhood experience provides an important frame of reference for the phenomenon of racial passing and the extent to which it is conditioned by ethnic and community norms regarding racial appearance. Early one morning Shelby becomes lost in the woods surrounding her house. She wanders to a different part of the island—the "white" part of Martha's Vineyard. Although an all-points bulletin has been issued, Shelby goes missing for most of the day because the search is for a lost colored child—and to the white residents, Shelby does not look colored. When a group of white mothers encounter Shelby, and one suggests she may be the lost child another scoffs, "God may have given some coloreds light skin but He never gave them blond hair. And those eyes!"[9] The Oval's response to Shelby's safe return is bittersweet, their joy overshadowed by a sobering realization that Shelby's white appearance can be a liability and that they, the adults, are powerless to protect her outside the sheltered enclave they have created.

Shelby's daylong experience of being lost in the liminal space between colored and white is a pivotal moment of race consciousness. In bed at the end of her traumatic day, she has a sleepy conversation with her great grandmother, asking a series of questions about race.

> "Gram, [...] am I colored?"
>
> Gram's expression did not change. "Yes," she said, because there was no other answer, and to qualify it would not alter the fact but only confuse a child who preferred the simple truth.
>
> Shelby's chest heaved with simple relief, not because she was black, but because she was something definite and now she knew what it was. But a thought occurred to her, and she was anxious again. "Is Liz colored?"
>
> "Yes."
>
> "And Mommy?"
>
> "Yes."
>
> "And Daddy?"
>
> "Yes."
>
> "Are you colored too?"
>
> "I'm your gram."
>
> The answer satisfied Shelby. All the people she loved were like herself. "Oh, Gram, I'm so glad we're all colored. A lady told me I was white."[10]

As an adult, Shelby flouts the conventions of both dominant society and the black elite through her interracial relationship. She is engaged to Meade Howell, a white jazz musician of modest middle-class origin. Shelby's parents (not to mention the denizens of the Oval) are dismayed that Shelby has chosen to squander her future with Meade when she could have had her pick of the eligible (colored) bachelors. Meade's parents' refusal to attend the wedding adds humiliation to the Coleses' distress, a reminder that to whites Ovalites are just as "colored" as Negroes of lower caste status.[11] As disappointed as the family are about Shelby's choice, not just any colored man would be a good alternative to Meade. Lute McNeil, a successful businessman renting a cottage on the island, has spent the summer attempting to gain acceptance from the residents of the Oval, to no avail. Both his lack of the appropriate family heritage and his dark skin condemn him to permanent outsider status. When Lute attempts to lure the virginal Shelby from her fiancé, it is both a matter of sexual attraction and a strategy to gain access to the class that has shunned him. The triangulation between Shelby, Meade, and Lute is a metaphor symbolizing the lethal combination of intra-racial prejudice and intolerance for interracial unions. For West, these forms of intolerance are analogous and equally destructive. In *The Wedding*, Shelby's body is both the battleground for these conflicts and the crucible within which they are ultimately, if provisionally, resolved. Crucially, *The Wedding* miniseries virtually ignores West's key themes of racial ambiguity and racial passing, which are expressed through Shelby's ambiguously raced body. This factor may be an effect of significant changes related to the meaning of race pride and the types of representations considered "positive" for a post–Civil Rights era television audience. The recuperation of an insular and privileged group of African Americans of the 1950s as a positive image for a 1990s television audience represents a significant—if not risky—shift in the politics of representation.

In addition to the internal struggles that members of the privileged classes may experience vis-à-vis blackness, they have been harshly criticized for promoting assimilation and a physical appearance reflecting mixed race. Louis Massiah's documentary of W. E. B. Du Bois relates Jamaican race leader Marcus Garvey's initial response upon walking into the NAACP offices in New York: "Where are the Negroes?" calling out the light-skinned and virtually white appearance of figures such as W. E. B. Du Bois and Walter White.[12] Garvey's question clearly implies visually intelligible blackness is a marker of racial authenticity. Garvey disparaged the bourgeois values of figures like Du Bois whose talented tenth would provide the ideal leadership for the African American masses. His challenges to early twentieth-century black intelligentsia points to a dilemma of racial authenticity for the black middle classes that became more acute as the twentieth century progressed.[13] William Julius Wilson argues the class divide separating the black middle class from other African Americans was, in the late twentieth century, more significant than the racial divide between black and white Americans.[14] Henry Louis Gates concurred in a television documentary focusing on how economically privileged African Americans struggle with the question of what links them to the large number of blacks whose socioeconomic conditions have changed little since the late 1960s.[15] Following the dismantling of affirmative action programs across the country, a move citing the black middle class as proof that such initiatives are no longer needed, white media have picked up on the debate about racial authenticity. Journalist Mike Wallace's question to Oprah Winfrey, "How black are you?" highlighted the association of blackness with the abject, a position at odds with the powerful role of black expressive culture in the late twentieth century.[16] Privileged African Americans "keep it real," or stabilize cultural identity, through vernacular speech and behaviors, a significant shift in how the black middle class engages in self-representation.[17]

The elite class in *The Wedding*, however, appropriates white middle class values of the period. Although contemporary African Americans may experience pride upon learning about the legacy of black professionals, middle-class ambivalence about racial identity is difficult to claim as empowering representation. The broadcast of *The Wedding* during African American History month positions it as a representative racial text targeting a black viewing audience. The ability to recognize oneself in representation has become a key feature of the demand among people of color for inclusion in media. The aesthetic appreciation of African heritage, expressed in Black Power's iconic phrase "Black is beautiful," is characterized by an inversion of the hierarchy of physical features that privileges light skin and so-called European features. Yet, the notion of a visually self-evident and thus empowering African heritage demands stable signifiers in visual representations. In this sense, racial ambiguity—the idea that race is not visually self-evident—conflicts with the notion of positive images of black Americans.

Changes made to *The Wedding*'s plot emphasize a notion of positive images reflecting late twentieth-century standards. Casting is one of the primary indicators, as Shelby and family are portrayed by light to medium brown-skinned African American actors. Considerably darker skinned actors play the roles of domestic servants and the interloper Lute McNeil. Early in the broadcast domestic workers in the Coleses' household gossip about their observation that the Oval's oldest families are all "high yellow."[18] In a telling scene Shelby's mother Corinne (played by Lynn Whitfield) ensures the bride figure on Shelby's wedding cake will be colored *and* light-skinned. The Coleses represent a range of colors, from Corinne's biracial yet only light-skinned colored, to Shelby's virtually white colored. Print stills promoting *The Wedding* communicated the triangulation between Shelby, Meade, and Lute through an image depicting the three actors as markers on a skin color continuum.[19] Light brown-skinned Halle Berry stands between her fiancé Meade, played by the pale-skinned Anglo-American Eric Thal, and her would-be suitor Lute McNeil, dark brown-skinned African American Carl Lumbly. The arrangement of the figures in the photograph effectively communicates the idea that Shelby's body signifies the space between the races rather than suggesting that she could easily be mistaken for a white woman. The promotional image of Lute, Shelby, and Meade fleshes out West's insightful depiction of the color line as a boundary between and within the races. Shelby signifies the line separating black and white and the caste hierarchy among African Americans.[20] Casting Halle Berry as a light-skinned but still identifiably black Shelby satisfies the imperative of a visually self-evident blackness and reifies the conventional notion of beauty for African American women.

The adaptation's elision of racial passing pivots on Halle Berry as Shelby, described in West's novel as blonde and blue-eyed—an incarnation of Gram in her youth. This is indeed the great-grandmother's appearance in the miniseries (as played by the actress Shirley Knight)—white skin, white hair, and pale blue eyes—making her stand out in a family of light brown-skinned and brown-eyed African Americans. Changing this element of the plot defuses one of West's key narrative tensions. West's virtually white African Americans beg the question, "What does blackness (not to mention whiteness) look like?" In the novel, the pivotal event in Shelby's childhood—becoming lost and unrecognizable in the white section of Martha's Vineyard—makes clear that Shelby's racial identity is a function of social and cultural belonging rather than physical appearance. In the miniseries, Shelby recounts the event with a very different emphasis.

> I was gone for the entire day. I had the whole Oval looking for me. There were reports going around the island that there was a lost little colored child. A policeman finally found me [and] brought me back to the Oval. And I was so happy to be home. 'Cause no more funny faces (were) staring at me asking me if I was that lost little colored child. I didn't even know what that meant at the time. But I sure found out.

Remarking that she is not sure why she has related this story to him, Meade responds by suggesting her memory is jarred by his parents' refusal to attend their wedding. As in the novel, the Coleses are, in the white world, as vulnerable to the indignities of colored status as any African Americans, regardless of color or class. However, the miniseries elides the liminal position that African Americans like the Coleses occupy generated by white-looking appearances in social life. In a subplot about the long-term affair between Shelby's father Clark and his mistress Rachel, white patrons of a restaurant assume they are an interracial couple composed of a white man and black woman.[21]

In the decades between *The Wedding*'s period setting and the novel's publication in 1995, black cultural nationalism intervened in the narrative characterizing interracial relationships as social progress, equating them instead with false consciousness and cultural genocide. Renée Romano writes: "By the 1970s, black students were boycotting black activist Julius Lester's classes at the University of Massachusetts because his wife was white, and LeRoi Jones, the black activist writer who changed his name to Amiri Baraka, left his white wife, unable to reconcile love across the racial divide with the struggle for black equality."[22]

West's novel challenges the idea that interracial relationships during slavery or in the post-bellum South were always a function of violence or coercion. Both Clark and Corinne trace their heritage to interracial relationships in the South diverging from these historical models. Although the pattern of rape and sexual exploitation of black women by white men is an inescapable historical reality, West's plot reminds us that there is also a history of less coercive, nonviolent, and even consensual interracial intimacy.

Some media reviews of *The Wedding* reveal a common oversimplification of the complex perspective of the mid-century's black elite toward intermarriage. In National Public Radio commentary prior to the broadcast, the reviewer reported the interracial marriage was "very important to the (Coles) family," implying that whereas the Coleses were pleased at the prospect of a "real" white son-in-law, contemporary black Americans reject interracial marriage.[23] The Coleses' perspective on whiteness is far more ambivalent, revealing less a desire to be white than a notion of race pride deeply incompatible with what it means to be black and proud today.[24]

The Wedding's literary and visual texts unambiguously assert the racial caste system has maintained the illusion of white racial purity through a segregation relying on interracial couples and people of mixed race remaining within African American communities. Several flashback scenes in the miniseries make clear the obsessive fixation on color hierarchies among elite African Americans is a direct effect of the one-drop rule and the struggle to assimilate its effects. At the same time, since *The Wedding* does not mourn the porous nature of African American racial boundaries, it opens a space for a multiracial audience to identify with its protagonists. The interracial relationships of the narrative are appropriate precursors to the consensual interracial relationships and marriages of the post-*Loving* United States society. In this regard, television viewers of the 1990s, for whom such relationships were increasingly normative, constituted a ripe audience for the romance between Shelby and Meade.

The Wedding's themes of family relations across racial lines and the arbitrariness of classification resonated with biracial memoirs of the 1990s. In West's novel, Shelby's mulatto/a body figures in a range of racialized discourses, and is claimed by different racialized imperatives. In the first instance, Shelby's upper-class family expects her to act as a vessel for the reproduction of an elite African American bloodline. For Gram, Shelby embodies a potential bridge back to whiteness. Early in the novel Gram fantasizes Shelby's "true white" marriage will reinvigorate the white blood in the family: "Shelby's hand . . . was being joined in marriage to a true white one, and that union, in the time of generations, would return to its origination, the colored blood drained out, degree by degree, until none was left, either known or remembered."[25] Gram's reverie is eerily reminiscent of Thomas Jefferson's ruminations about race in an 1815 letter to Francis C. Gray. In response to Gray's question regarding whether a "mulatto" was Negro or white, Jefferson delineated a complex algebraic formula designed to calculate the relative proportions of white and Negro blood in individuals resulting from race mixture over several generations. He concludes, "Our canon considers two crosses with the pure white and a third with any degree of mixture, however small, as clearing the issue of the negro blood."[26]

Ultimately, the novel celebrates Shelby's body as a bridge between the races when she emerges from the doubts seeded by her fleeting attraction to Lute McNeil. Shelby "makes the leap between the races" because, West explains, "The scales had fallen from her eyes. All of Lute's words about remaining true to one's race, all his subtle slurs, his sly digs, all were lies, pretexts . . . Color was a false distinction; love was not."[27]

This passage articulates one of the novel's most important themes—the prejudicial values which impel elite light-skinned African Americans to choose each other as mates are analogous to the segregationist values that compel people to marry within racial lines. West's narrative expresses a plea for the power of love seeking harmony and union rather than the preservation of racial status and the possibility of social class mobility. Oprah Winfrey's introduction to part two of the miniseries explicitly refers to this theme when she states Shelby and the Coles family will "learn the folly of decisions based on false values rather than love."

The romance of *The Wedding* miniseries derives from its resolution— Shelby and Meade's triumphant union. The closing shot is a portrait of the Coles family on the day of the wedding. Shelby's final voiceover paraphrases West's words: "Color is a false distinction and so is class—love is not." *The Wedding* perpetuates the comforting narrative suggesting that individuals can dismantle racism through personal transformation. To communicate this message, the extra-diegetic media of the miniseries focused on post–Civil Rights mixed race. Following broadcasts of the miniseries, news media featured stories of interracial couples and families, and mixed-race people. Halle Berry as Shelby was a crucial factor for her ability to signify as a black/white woman—as both as a figure of identification for African Americans and symbol of mixed race in the present and future.

In *The Wedding* Dorothy West describes the reaction of an elderly white couple that Shelby encounters the day she is lost. Like the other white residents of the island, they cannot see Shelby's blackness, and therefore do not wonder whether she might be the missing colored child. West writes: "They said they had not seen her, and watched the searchers go off. In a way, they were better off not knowing how unhelpful they had been, and better off not knowing that they had glimpsed in Shelby the overlapping worlds and juxtaposed mores they would not live to see."[28]

West's "overlapping worlds and juxtaposed mores" are embodied in Berry, considered an exemplary African American actress and role model, with known biracial heritage. In her film roles Berry's image is not fixed on the representational radar; rather she oscillates between characters including authentic black woman and tragic mulatto.[29] Being cast in differently racialized roles—white, black, and mixed—is not a function of Berry's physical appearance. Rather, the narrative and technical aspects of mise-en-scene—namely lighting, costume, styling—as well as the actors cast opposite Berry—shape the impression of racial identity. *The Wedding*'s screenplay does not raise the possibility that members of the Coles family look white, instead using terms such as high yellow to focus on skin-color hierarchies. Shelby's sister Liz questions her motivations for marrying Meade, asking, "Is that why you're marrying a white man? So that you'll have light-skinned children?" A similar conversation between Liz and Shelby explicitly engages racial passing. The passage begins with Shelby:

> "Liz, what if I don't have the strength to fight a war against bigotry every day of my life, for myself and for my children?"
>
> "What if you don't?" Liz answered impatiently. "Do you really expect an answer to that question? If you're that worried about it, why don't you just pass?"
>
> Shelby recoiled as if struck. "You have to be kidding."
>
> "Why? You could, you know, you easiest of all of us. Don't tell me you've never thought about it. Meade has a hard enough road in front of him without taking on the cross of your color."
>
> "Don't be a fool. And live my life in shame and embarrassment, always being scared of being exposed? I think not."
>
> "Come on Shelby, don't be so naïve."
>
> "No, you come on Liz. I would never do that to my children."[30]

By implicitly posing the question, "What is the meaning of racial passing?" West's novel poses a conundrum about racial visibility and intelligibility. By contrast, because the miniseries implies that race is self-evident, it reifies racial classification even as, through the celebration of interracial marriage, it points to a future present with the potential to undermine the logic of racial categories. The historical setting of 1953 calls for a scenario that anticipates rather than represents the significant social changes shaped in part by rising rates of interracial marriage. Those themes were explored in the cultural and media context of the broadcast.

Nightly news shows following broadcasts of *The Wedding* in California featured segments about interracial couples and families and mixed-race people from a variety of ethnic backgrounds. Census 2000 indicates that California's self-identified multiracial population is nearly twice the national average.[31] The stories of couples and families highlighted the improved social climate as well as challenges persisting nearly forty years after the time period of *The Wedding*. These broadcasts differed markedly from Oprah Winfrey's characterization of *The Wedding* as a history lesson about the professional, elite class of African Americans—a legacy of which to be proud. The media focused rather on mixed race as the harbinger, if not the vanguard of a necessary social transformation in race relations.

The representational emphasis on interracial relationships between black and white Americans, and on the black/white figure, is striking given statistically low rates of interracial marriage and the low number of biracial African Americans electing to identify as mixed race. This contradiction points to a symbolic power of racial dualism related to marriage and self-identified multiracial people. Biracial individuals of the post–Civil Rights period tend to be included among, as well as to identify with, African Americans. Many of them express a dual identity in which being black and being mixed are not mutually exclusive. However, African Americans regard biracial people with ambivalence. On one hand, this is due to the way in which black Americans have adopted the standard of the one-drop rule. This phenomenon has engendered a practice of policing racial boundaries in an inverse fashion. That is to say, rather than an effort to keep biracial people (who might be considered racially impure) out of the group, there is instead not only a tendency to include them, but also to direct hostility at those who do not explicitly identify as black. Mariah Carey and golf pro Tiger Woods, hesitant to identify exclusively as African American, have been the subjects of considerable derision.[32] The refusal to identify as African American—whether by explicit statement or passive omission—is equated with historical efforts made by individuals and groups able to avoid being classified as black.[33] While such strategies could be justified under conditions of institutional racial inequality, African Americans of today are far less likely to be complicit in racial passing.

On the other hand, despite an apparent attachment to the one-drop rule, contemporary African Americans also police racial boundaries according to visual interpretations of racial appearance. Adrian Piper meticulously explores the socio-psychological freight accompanying the process of identifying someone's racial heritage according to the "evidence" of physical features. As she argues, the interpretation of a person's so-called race on the basis of the visual is a subjective process naturalized.[34] Prime-time products such as *The Wedding* are strongly invested in the unambiguous representation of racial appearance—a necessity for positive racial images. This priority makes visual intelligibility a standard of representation and as such a characteristic equated with racial authenticity. The question of physical features, and whether an individual's appearance reflects so-called race mixing, is crucial because racially ambiguous people are, for African American communities, symbolic of a heterogeneity that is a constant reminder of the impossibility of keeping black racial boundaries intact. The significance of the woman's body as a point of entry, if you will, for this racial difference—on a material level (her biological, reproductive function) as well as on a metaphorical, representational level—accounts for the ways writers and filmmakers continuously return to the theme of the (potentially tragic) mulatto. The ambivalent stance the black elite of *The Wedding* expresses toward whiteness—a position articulated in both the novel and the miniseries—is clearly present in contemporary representations of black/white women in visual culture.

Halle Berry appeared on *Oprah* in a segment timed to promote *The Wedding*.[35] Berry, a multifaceted bridging figure, is an ideal casting choice to portray Shelby. Just as West elaborates the ways that Shelby can be interpellated by a variety of racialized discourses, Berry's mixed-race female body is also highly malleable. Berry's beauty is consistent with a mulatto/a aesthetic making her, like the fictional Shelby, a symbolic index on the color line between and within the races. As the child of an interracial marriage, Berry bridges the 1950s setting of the narrative and its extra-diegetic gesture toward a post–Civil Rights future. Berry's simultaneous articulation of her black identity and acknowledgment of her biracial heritage expresses an important transition in what the mulatto/a signifies to a late twentieth-century society. In the 1990s, the black/white figure transcended the status of tragic figure to become a proudly hybrid African American, no longer subject to the humiliating imperative to pass in order to fulfill her potential. The discussion about *The Wedding* on *Oprah* reiterated the focus of the miniseries, plumbing the topic of color hierarchies among African Americans and drawing the analogy with racial conflict and taboos against interracial marriage—a topic that Berry engaged from her personal standpoint. Overall, the *Oprah* discourse drew upon the narrative of *The Wedding* to argue for the value of color blindness, an ideological position that resolves both intra-racial and interracial tensions in the story.

As Henry Louis Gates wrote in a eulogy for West, she persisted in calling African Americans colored people; for her the designation most appropriately described the range of physical types in the community.[36] For West, color blindness is not about willfully ignoring difference, but understanding that visually apparent differences are, to use a colloquial phrase, no more than skin deep. In *The Wedding*, West extends this conviction to critique the practice of racial passing. She departs from traditional passing narratives by de-emphasizing the moral dilemma of deliberate passing to expose the nuances undergirding what might be called unintentional passing—an individual becoming the site of projections shaped by assumptions about race conditioned by ethnic and cultural norms. For the miniseries, the goal of being a representative television product for African Americans necessitates unambiguous, visually intelligible blackness.

It is productive to put *The Wedding* into conversation with its television miniseries adaptation to explore some of the stakes involved in translating works of literature for mass audiences. The miniseries eviscerates themes of racial passing and racial ambiguity that West explores in her novel because these topics pose representational challenges for the visual medium of television. Contemporary media remain strongly influenced by values which emerged during the Civil Rights and Black Power movements, emphasizing the importance of disseminating positive images of African Americans. This imperative has become conflated with the notion that racial difference is—or at least should be—discernible through visual evidence. The representation of West's putatively white-looking character Shelby as the light-skinned but identifiably black character portrayed by Halle Berry highlights the complex stakes involved in the appropriation of African American literature for mass media. In a medium that must communicate coherent narratives to diverse audiences, the lack of fixed determinants of racial identity can be a liability. By contrast, West's novel frankly engages the conundrum of racial visibility and racial passing in a critique exposing the utter unreliability of visual evidence in determining racial identity. For West, race and color are metaphors for Shelby's cultural identity as a member of a socioeconomically privileged African American family with a multiracial and multiethnic heritage.

Both versions of *The Wedding* identify Shelby's body as a figure that disrupts the belief that color is a reliable marker of race. When femininity is brought into the equation, Shelby resists the pre-determined path for women of her class and caste. Shelby is a multidimensional symbol. She embodies the privileged mulatto/a aesthetic and represents historical race mixture in African American families, a genetically hybrid heritage anticipating the increasing number of interracial marriages and self-consciously identified mixed-race individuals emergent in the 1990s. Shelby's dilemma of marriage to Meade—whether it involves the consideration of racial passing, the disapproval of her family, or the specter of white hostility, implicitly gestures backward toward literary narratives of the tragic mulatto. By casting the biracial yet black-identified actress Halle Berry in the role of Shelby, the miniseries bridges the novel's historicized rendering of intra-racial and interracial tensions of the 1950s with the time period of the 1990s, in which interracial couples and biracial people are increasingly familiar. Like Shelby, Halle Berry represents the ambiguity of the color line, its dual nature, and most of all the potential of the female body to destabilize racial boundaries. By the same token, Berry symbolizes a transitional moment for the black/white woman in popular culture, embodying a vexed condition, but not necessarily a tragic one. The miniseries is explicit about being a positive representation of African Americans broadcast during Black History Month, as well as engaging the theme of interracial love in a celebratory fashion befitting Valentine's Day. Extra-diegetic media featuring actual interracial couples and biracial people, along with *Oprah* reinforce the message that black and biracial identity are not mutually exclusive. And yet, the black/white woman's liminal position is not fully resolved—caught in the web of normative discourses of race—whiteness as a function of purity, the demand for black authenticity, and the naturalized expectation that race is visually self-evident.

As a dual text in popular culture, *The Wedding* in its narrative movement between books and films foregrounds the politics of ambiguity. The bodies of black/white women in literary text and on screen are figures of identification and commodification. The media's forging of a relationship between the mulatto figure then and mixed-race people now demonstrates popular culture's grasp of relationships between historical mixed race among African Americans and the post-*Loving* social formations of interracial families and mixed-race identities.

CHAPTER 3
Sex and Femininity in Danzy Senna's Novels

Danzy Senna's novel *Caucasia* revises the classic mulatto/a dilemmas of passing and racial authenticity in the historical terrain of 1970s American culture, against the backdrop of Black Nationalism and anti-establishment political activism pursued by groups such as the Weather Underground. *Caucasia*'s narrative depicts how interracial marriages and mixed-race children fare in socially progressive environments, parsing contradictions in radical ideologies. Movements for social justice are not exempt from conventional racial polarization. Interracial couples and mixed-race children can be marginalized, albeit along a different ideological rationale. Racial valorization in Black Nationalism and Afrocentrism emphasize a return to idealized traditional masculinities, femininities, and the black family, cultural priorities leaving little space for white wives—however enlightened they might be—and white-looking mixed-race children.[1] This 1970s cultural moment suspended the conventional practice of black communities "absorbing" interracial families. These circumstances, along with the white community's habitual rejection of women married to black men, compound social isolation, and as *Caucasia* depicts, add extra stress to the already challenging obstacles interracial couples face.[2] In the novel, racial polarization seeps into intimate life, resulting in the novel's affecting portrait of a young black/white girl's coming of age while passing as white.

Senna's novel opens in polarized Boston of the 1970s, a decade characterized by white backlash against the legal gains of the Civil Rights era,
represented in that city by vicious opposition to the controversial practice
of busing designed to integrate the city's public schools. During this same
period, Black Nationalism was emerging as a response to the nonviolent
civil disobedience actions that successfully challenged Jim Crow segregation. The first-person voice of the novel belongs to Birdie Lee, a biracial girl whose parents, Deck and Sandy, have a marriage that is falling
apart in a way intensified by a mutual alienation based on politics. Deck's
adoption of Black Nationalism represents a struggle to reconcile an elite
education with his membership in the black community. For Deck, Black
Power is less about activism than about remaking himself as an authentic
black man. Sandy, the daughter of Deck's Harvard philosophy professor,
has spent her adult life distancing herself from an exemplary blue-blood
background, most recently becoming immersed in radical, illegal activi-
ties. Although Deck and Sandy's relationship has long been volatile, the
death throes of their marriage are hastened by Deck's appropriation of
Nationalist standards of race loyalty and black authenticity. He attributes
their marital conflict to racial difference and the doomed nature of interracial unions, while Sandy lambastes him for his superficial attempts to
deny his "honkified past." Their polarization reflects Black Nationalism's
counter-discourse to the Civil Rights focus on interracial coalitions and
the liberal notion of biracial babies as symbols of a utopian multiracial
future. Although Deck regards Birdie and her sister Cole as interesting
mulatto/a objects of inquiry, neither he nor Sandy idealizes their daughters' race mixture.

The mixed-race child as the product of "Freedom Summer" (1964) and
later 1970s encounters between black men and white women engaged in
shared political struggle is a controversial figure weighted with inflam-
matory meanings. One way of looking at Freedom Summer is as "the
summer of love" for interracial couples in the South. For most Southerners, Freedom Summer materialized the dreaded specter of uncontrolled
miscegenation. The belief that miscegenation—symbolized by the innocent mixed-race child—will bring an end to racial tension[3] battles with
the particularly southern notion of miscegenation—black male access
to white women—as the primary objective of the diabolical plan of
black struggle for equality—especially integration. W. E. B. Du Bois's

reminder "we do not seek amalgamation" expresses the tension between black desire to re-impose racial boundaries (and the particularly male investment in them) and the view of miscegenation law as critical to the apparatus of white supremacy.

Black women's representations of how black men assert their masculinity in Civil Rights and Black Power struggles—in Alice Walker's *Meridian,* for example—foreground the way patriarchal entitlement can be an expression of progressive ideological stances such as Nationalism and the resistance to white supremacy. When Walker's protagonist Meridian first encounters Truman in college, she becomes the potential vessel for "his black babies" and thus his Afro-centrism, his authentic blackness. Later, he leaves Meridian for the white, Northern, and Jewish activist Lynn; they marry and have a child. When Truman eventually rejects Lynn, Walker frames his actions as misogynistic—he tells Lynn she is fat and ugly. Toward the end of the novel, Lynn discovers Truman's lover is a tiny blonde southern girl—Lynn calls her "Miss Scarlett." The final depiction of Truman conforms to Michele Wallace's contention that Black Nationalist men assert masculinity through sexual liaisons with white women characterized as attacks on the white power structure.

Senna signifies upon the capricious nature of genetic heritage through "blood sisters" Birdie and Cole, who while possessing identical "percentages" of racial heritage appear so different that not even their parents are immune to treating them as if they are fundamentally different racial beings. The sisters inhabit positions on extreme ends of the visual spectrum within blackness, the virtually white versus the visibly black. Their appearance is testimony to the ways black/white bodies thwart the practice of linking percentages of blood and appearance, where diminishing black heritage—a successive generational distance from African ancestors—is equated with progressive lightening of skin and Anglicization of features.[4] In Nella Larsen's novels, *Quicksand*'s biracial and light brown-skinned Helga Crane cannot pass as white, whereas Clare Kendry of *Passing,* with just one white grandparent, passes effectively enough to disappear into a white marriage.[5] Likewise, *The Wedding*'s Shelby looks "more white" than her biracial mother Corrine. These dissonances between fractions of blood and appearance inform identity. Deck's ambiguous relationship to blackness is, tellingly, associated with physical ambiguity and multiracial heritage. Sandy's memory of her first impression of Deck squares with Jack D. Forbes's argument about the understudied results of Native American heritage among African Americans:[6] Deck "was not very dark and his features were not very African . . . his face spoke of something other—his high cheekbones, his large bony nose, his deep-set eyes, and his thin lips against the brown of his skin . . . His hair wasn't so wooly either."[7]

The not-so-wooly texture of Deck's hair marks him in ways related to black authenticity as style and as racial (im)purity. Hair took on particular significance in popular images of the Black Power movement, when along with the raised fist the Afro—the bigger the better—became a penultimate symbol of pride and cultural identity. Although hairstyles were important in the representation of black women,[8] the Afro was also prevalent in the depiction of male nationalist icons such as Huey Newton of the Black Panthers. Yet the Afro eluded many African Americans who simply did not possess the hair texture suited to the style. Deck, Senna has Birdie say, "had kept his afro short. It wasn't nappy enough to get really big . . . my father tried growing it big one year and it looked funny. Someone . . . patted it, giggled, and said, 'Man, you got a Jewfro!'"[9]

Birdie's memory of Deck's "Jewfro" surfaces as she discusses her phantom Jewish father with the Marshes in New Hampshire. Here Jewishness as an alterity analogous to blackness threatens to expose Birdie rather than provide the cover enabling her to pass.[10] Hair texture also constitutes a critical physical difference between Birdie and Cole—just as important as their skin color in locating them on opposite ends of the black/white continuum: "[Cole's] hair was curly and mine was straight, and I figured that this fact must have something to do with [Deck and Sandy's] fighting and the way the eyes of strangers flickered surprise, sometimes amusement, sometimes disbelief when my mother introduced us as sisters."[11]

Deck solidifies his tenuous link to blackness through Cole, the daughter whose features are more black than his own. As Senna emphasizes, Cole's body materializes a concrete—and reassuring—connection to blackness for Deck. Birdie reflects:

> Cole was his proof that he had indeed survived the integrationist shuffle, that he had remained human despite what seemed a conspiracy to turn him into stone. She was his proof of the pudding, his milk-chocolate pudding, the small dusky body, the burst of mischievous curls (nappier

> than his own) the full pouting lips (fuller than his own).
> Her existence told him that he hadn't wandered quite
> so far and that his body still held the power to leave its
> mark. He usually treated me with a cheerful disinterest.[12]

Deck's relationship with Birdie is dissonant to those who see race as blood boundary. A couple watching Deck and Birdie in a public park, alarmed at seeing a little white girl child with a black man, alert police officers. This encounter reinforces Deck and Sandy's rationale of splitting up their children along racial lines when they decide to separate. Deck's interracial marriage and family expose him to the dangers inherent in transgressing boundaries in a racially charged environment. As in the real-life example of LeRoi Jones, who remade himself as an Afro-centric intellectual after leaving Hettie Jones, complete with marriage to an African American woman, Sandy constitutes a potential impediment to Deck's political legitimacy and acceptance as an authentic African American. While Deck is too critical of the racial classification system to effect a transformation such as Jones's, he temporarily enjoys the sense of belonging he derives from his relationship with Carmen (his "brown sugar") and the short-lived fantasy of moving with Carmen and Cole to what he believes to be the "racial paradise" of Brazil.

The spectacle of the visual constitutes the lynchpin of the novel, for when the parents decide to separate, the family splits precisely on the color line. While Sandy's maternal relationship to Cole is unintelligible as familial, once exposed as a "race traitor" she is vulnerable to hostility and being characterized as a perversely sexual white woman—willfully impure and out of control. Sandy explicitly links her participation in radical politics and the risky illegal action that precipitates her going underground to being the mother of Cole, her "black child." Yet the hyper-visibility of the interracial relation compels Sandy to pass as an "untainted" white woman, leaving Cole with Deck and effecting a reincarnation of Birdie as Sandy's not-quite-white (because half-Jewish) daughter. Crucially, both Deck and Sandy ground their identification with blackness in Cole's racialized body. In this sense, both parents play out Birdie's worst fears of being trapped in a body that not only masks but also negates her black identity.

In *Caucasia*, Senna uses ethnicity to expose historical contradictions and instabilities of white identity. The multitude of ethnic types other characters conjure to name Birdie evokes precisely the historical "thickness" of ethnicity and the complex and contradictory nature in which it is enmeshed with race. Birdie's multiplicity makes her at least four girls; the ambiguity that attends her proper name is the first line of fragmentation. To her father, she is Patrice for Congolese martyr Patrice Lumumba, to Cole she is Birdie, a surrogate for a pet bird, and to Sandy she is Jesse for Sandy's suffragette grandmother. Being also the half-Jewish girl Sandy concocts on the lam, Jesse is a dual identity. Moreover, this latter Jesse splits again in terms of sexuality: both the pre-pubescent girl who experiences initiation into sexual desire with another girl (Alex, her friend at the women's commune), and the young teenager who considers giving up her virginity to Nicholas, the WASP wet dream. During sexual play with Nicholas Jesse fragments once more as Birdie emerges to rebel against sex with a white boy.

Birdie's resemblance to "a little Sicilian" (Sandy), "a Guinea" (Redbone), and a "Byzantine icon" (Libby Marsh) is a reflection of European types become synonymous with whiteness. The kaleidoscopic possibilities of Birdie's body point to the many fissures within the imaginary land of "Caucasia." Although people from the Indian continent are included in this anthropological group, dark skin color problematizes their status as white. "India" is redolent of the exotic, as Birdie is fully aware when she tells a group of young children she is a kidnapped Indian princess named "Tanzania."[13] And as case law makes clear, for most of U.S. history whereas Indians have been acknowledged as Caucasian (or Aryan), courts decline to declare that they are white.[14]

Jewish people have long constituted an enigma for anthropological classification; they are a diasporic, multiracial, and multiethnic people with origins in the Middle East, but historically their religious beliefs are the a priori basis for their racialization. Although many Jews, particularly non-practicing, have assimilated as white in the United States, Jesse's encounter with anti-Semitism in New Hampshire—being called a "kike"—indicates how uneven assimilation has been. Finally, Birdie's dark body invokes another Indian princess, "Pocahontas," for Nicholas Marsh. Tellingly, the novel alludes to the racialized and hierarchical difference between northern and southern European ethnicities when, on separate occasions, Birdie's grandmother and Libby Marsh remark she "could *even* be French" (my emphasis), an indication of her less probable but possible resemblance to a more desirable European group—not the ideal Anglo-Saxon pedigree but far away enough from Africa and culturally impressive to boot.[15]

In the novel, then, Birdie simultaneously inhabits the three "races of man" identified by physical anthropologists: Caucasian (European), Mongoloid (American Indian), and Negroid. Yet, because the one-drop rule boils American Negroes down to race alone, in the United States blacks must, in general, pass in order to possess ethnicity. Birdie, however, whose body is so malleable to ethnic identities, encounters significant resistance from African Americans who cannot see her blackness. Birdie's lived reality—a white appearance trumping the one-drop rule—indicates that a "tipping point" exists somewhere on the spectrum between virtual whiteness and visible blackness. One of John Gwaltney's subjects in a study of black Americans makes the point: "Black people are all colors. White people don't all look the same way, but there are many more different kinds of us than there are of them. Then too, there is a certain stage at which you cannot tell who is white and who is black."[16] The idea of a tipping point complicates the structural norm of dualism and the rhetoric of passing; both of which depend upon the acceptance of discernible, reliable boundaries. My use of the term understands a tipping point as a moment in space and time that precedes the forward movement—an ephemeral transitional temporality during which the terms of intelligibility change.

Birdie's coming of age is marked by participation in racialized rites of girlhood,[17] first at an Afro-centric school in Boston, and later in the conservative white setting of small-town New Hampshire while passing as "Jesse Goldman." These rituals of black and white girlhood frame critical transitions in *Caucasia*, both in the construction of Birdie's self-identity and the way others perceive her racial identity. In effect, Birdie passes for black and for white through an explicit process of gendering. Although these performative rituals should stabilize Birdie's sense of self, a fixed racial identity does not necessarily translate to heteronormative femininity.

As a pre-teen at the Nkrumah School, Birdie is initially miserable because her light skin and straight hair make her stand out among the children. When she is asked to declare, "Black is Beautiful" in her class, Birdie is teased, "Guess you must be ugly."[18] Birdie's strategy for survival at Nkrumah includes masking her hair texture by wearing it pulled back and tightly braided, and practicing black vernacular at home. She is harassed by girls in the school bathroom who accuse her of thinking she's "all that" because she's white—and they threaten to cut off her hair. In this scene, the girls enact a familiar rite among African American girls whose competition is complicated by the ways features are racialized and, even in a Black Nationalist school, long straight hair is a desirable attribute. When Cole defends Birdie, telling the girls, "Birdie isn't white. She's black. Just like me," the ringleader Maria responds, "So now I know."[19] Cole's assimilation to blackness is less bumpy, but she learns to use lotion after being teased for having ashy skin, and convinces her father to send her to a hair salon to get a cornrow style.

Birdie's experience at Nkrumah improves dramatically once Ali—the boy who teased her about being ugly—singles her out as attractive. Subsequently she is befriended by Maria (her former nemesis), who invites her to become a member of the "Brown Sugars"—a club for girls with boyfriends. Birdie does not understand what Maria means when she tells her, "I got a brother just like you. We're Cape Verdean."[20] The comment references heterogeneity in the black diaspora that is masked by the one-drop rule. Cape Verde, a group of islands in the Atlantic west of Senegal, has a multiracial population that is the result of legacies of colonization as well as being a crossroads for a multitude of ethnic groups. Thus Maria's black identity is constituted through difference. In Maria's home, Birdie sees a photo of her brother, "a boy with hazel eyes and skin the color of my own." Birdie's rites of black girlhood include having her hair curled, learning to apply make-up, and changing her wardrobe. Yet, her transition to being a black girl remains colored by her difference. When Luce Rivera, a girl Birdie's age, is kidnapped and killed, Birdie's mother warns, "Don't ever go into Franklin Park alone. You hear me Bird? You be careful in Roxbury. Don't talk to anyone except your school friends. You understand? There are perverts, crazies, dirty old men, and they want little girls like you."[21] The idea that Birdie would be vulnerable in Roxbury, a black section of Boston, points to the ways that girls and women experience racialized sexual violence. That a sexual predator would seek out a girl with a specific look indicates that racialization is fundamentally intertwined with projections having to do with gender and sexuality.

As Jesse Goldman, Birdie Lee assumes a "half-Jewish" heritage explaining her dark features without impugning Sandy's whiteness. In the New Hampshire town where they settle after four years on the road, Jesse experiences the rituals of assimilation into white teenage girlhood among the working-class trailer denizens who become her friends in junior high school. In an incident paralleling her experience at the Nkrumah School,

Jesse encounters hostile girls in the bathroom. She wins them over by claiming to be friends with Nicholas Marsh, the high school-age son of the Wasp couple from whom Sandy rents a cottage—thus, as at Nkrumah, ensuring her acceptance through masculine approval. Birdie becomes best friends with Mona, and her initiation into white girlhood involves listening to rock music, and learning to feather her hair and use hot pink blush and sparkly blue eye shadow. Sandy's transformation into an unmarked white woman is also shaped by her assimilation to heteronormative sexuality when she finds a white boyfriend, Jim. The more comfortable Sandy becomes in her relationship with him, the more Birdie chafes at passing, particularly when it begins to appear that the three of them are headed toward a nuclear family formation. Increasingly, Birdie's virtually white appearance—the straight hair and light skin that enable Sandy to remain safe from detection—lulls the mother into believing they can fully assimilate in New Hampshire. Sandy seems to forget Birdie is black/white—behaving as if Birdie's virtually white appearance immunizes her to the everyday racism Sandy would never expect her visibly black daughter Cole to withstand.

Black/white women in fictional narratives often inhabit a visual binary within the racial binary. Physical appearance falls into the visual dualism of "looking"—looking white and looking black. Virtually white appearance drives the pathos of archetypal tragic mulatta characters. These narratives of white-looking women imperiled by the drop of blood lurking under the skin stretch across time and genre. In *Clotel; or, The President's Daughter* (1853),[22] William Wells Brown fictionalized the rumor of Thomas Jefferson's mulatta daughter. In 1934 the film *Imitation of Life* introduced film audiences to Peola, a girl whose determination to pass permanently into the white world breaks her dark-skinned mother's heart.[23] Depicted by actress Fredi Washington, Peola became popular culture's touchstone for this troubled passing figure.

Birdie has more in common with a tougher mulatta character—Nella Larsen's Clare of *Passing* (1929). Though the novel ends with Clare's death, Larsen's tale anticipates nuances that render *Caucasia* compelling. Larsen broke new ground by portraying how the secret of racial passing incorporates the enticement of sexual taboo. In *Passing* Clare's white husband eroticizes the wife he believes is white by imagining she is black. In the following passage he explains the nickname he has given Clare:

"Hello Nig" . . . "Tell them dear, why you call me that."
. . . "Well you see, its like this. When we were first married, she was as white as—as—well as white as a lily.
But I declare she's gettin' darker and darker. I tell her
if she don't look out, she'll wake up one of these days
and find she's turned into a nigger." [. . .] "My goodness
Jack! What difference would it make if, after all these
years, you were to find out that I was one or two percent
coloured?" "Oh no, Nig," he declared, "nothing like that
with me. I know you're no nigger, so it's all right. You can
get as black as you please."[24]

As Birdie becomes assimilated to New Hampshire, her passing body
also becomes a tantalizing fetish for the teenagers in her world. The fantasy of Jesse's blackness is titillating as long as her friends believe she is
white. One afternoon they discuss the pursuit of suntans: "Dawn pitched
in: 'Shit. We're gonna look like little niggers if we stay out in the sun any
longer. Especially you, Jesse.' Mona looked me up and down, then said
with a laugh, 'Shit, Jess. You never burn. What's your secret?'"[25]

The fact that Birdie cannot "remember to forget"[26] her blackness leads
to lapses in the passing charade. While browsing a Tintin comic in Nicholas's bedroom, she instinctively reacts to a depiction of the Congolese.
Without thinking, she remarks: "They've made us look like animals."
Nicholas replies in a fashion similar to Clare's husband, fantasizing about
her blackness even as he dismisses it: "You said us . . . Shit, maybe you
could be colored in the right light. Better stay out of the sun." He smiled
slightly, and pushed some hair out of my face. "I was just kidding about
you looking colored. I mean, you don't look it at all. You're [. . .] pretty."[27]

As in the classic passing tales, for Birdie to be accepted as Jesse Goldman, all contact with blackness must be disavowed—a phenomenon
Birdie experiences as an amputation. And, as in passing narratives, the
presence of black people in one's immediate vicinity triggers an almost
unendurable, intertwined repulsion and desire. For Birdie, this person
is her classmate Samantha Taper, the adopted daughter of white parents
and "black like me. Half, that is . . . [b]ut her blackness was visible."[28]

Unable to articulate how Samantha affects her, Birdie keeps the secret
of the girl's existence from her mother Sandy, leading to an unexpected
encounter illuminating the steep price exacted for white privilege. Sandy

sees Samantha for the first time while shopping in a grocery store, experiencing a shock causing her to momentarily lose her equilibrium and grip on the alternate reality she has constructed for herself and Birdie. Mona makes a typically snide comment about Samantha, and Birdie, in the persona of Jesse, echoes her contempt. Sandy is outraged.

> My mother's voice sounded thick as she said, "A loser? Jesse Goldman, I never thought I'd hear you talk that way about another human being . . . that girl is no different from you."
>
> "You mean we're both black?" It had come out before I could stop it.
>
> My mother breathed in sharply . . . I heard Mona beginning to giggle . . . my mother put her hand to her temple, as if to stop a migraine. Then she began to giggle as well, loudly, in a way that made even Mona's smile disappear.[29]

The hysteria surfacing in Sandy's laughter is an effect of the pressure to hide the open secret constituted by the passing body—the hidden blackness invisible even when naked to the gaze. This undercurrent of hysteria is a continuous theme in the passing narrative: the uncontrolled laughter that erupts when subterfuge becomes simultaneously too absurd and too painful to bear.

Nella Larsen ends the passage explaining Clare's nickname "Nig" with a similar collapse into hysterical laughter that turns troubling. Here too the hysteria is a function of the pressure of the secret as experienced by the character Irene. Although Irene does not pass as a way of life, she and Gertrude are passing in this scene.

> [John Bellew] roared with laughter . . . Clare's ringing bell-like laughter joined his. Gertrude after another uneasy shift in her seat added her own shrill one. Irene, who had been sitting with lips tightly compressed, cried out: "That's good!" and gave way to gales of laughter. She laughed and laughed and laughed. Tears ran down her cheeks. Her sides ached. Her throat hurt. She laughed on and on and on, after the others had subsided. Until, catching sight of Clare's face, the need for a more quiet

enjoyment of this priceless joke, and for caution, struck
her. At once she stopped.

In *Passing* Clare's death is an ambiguous affair. Her desire to pass back, to
re-inhabit her blackness is a triple threat, endangering herself, her husband's
secure white identity, and her friend Irene's peace of mind. In Nella Larsen's
hands, Clare's mysterious death poses more questions than it answers. The
play of desire and attraction in *Passing* anticipates the clarity Danzy Senna
brings to the sexual dimensions of racial passing in *Caucasia.*

Ultimately, Samantha's presence and the racial visibility making her a
clear embodiment of the color line compel Birdie to abandon Jesse and
rediscover the racial alterity she has long repressed, to reclaim her kin-
ship with her sister: "That face that was me." In a moment materializing
Birdie's genuine coming of age, she believes she hears Samantha echo
the words Cole once spoke to rescue her from being harassed by girls at
the Nkrumah School: "She's black. Just like me."[30] Samantha's words to
Birdie, "I'm black. Like you" (286), is the exchange that finally frees Birdie
to follow her instincts and go in search of her father and Cole.

As Jesse, Birdie inherits a dual personality; named for Sandy's suffragette
grandmother and reborn as half-Jewish Jesse Goldman. As a passing figure,
Jesse experiences the confusing phenomenon of being treated as if she is
white (i.e., a person of value) and thus develops genuine affection for peers
like Mona and Nicholas. In order to survive Birdie must ignore both her
friends' racism and the inexorable way in which she feels drawn to Samantha—not to mention purging her memory of Cole and Deck. This disavowal
of one's black family is the most frequently cited reason for why, in history,
more "white-looking" African Americans have not passed—contrary to the
palpable fear of the phenomenon on the part of whites.[31]

For Birdie, the imperative to pass precipitates a multiple splitting along
the fault lines of gender and sexuality, as experiencing sexual coming of age
as a site imbued with racial meaning. Although Birdie has nascent sexual
interest in girls—from her fascination with Maria's body to later masturba-
tory games with Alexis at the women's commune—this desire is bracketed
as isolated experience having little to do with the "real world," where male
desire renders her sexually attractive and constitutes her as an appropriately
gendered subject. Just as Ali's selection of her as his "girlfriend" paved the
way for her being recruited by the "Brown Sugars," Birdie's interactions

with Nicholas facilitate her assimilation among the girls in New Hampshire. By the same token, burgeoning sexual curiosity leads her to consider how sexual practices impact her racial identity. When Birdie "necks" with Nicholas in his bedroom, she encounters the obstacle of his racism, becoming like Adrian Piper's unwilling witness under the most intimate of circumstances[32]—an experience even more alienating than the quotidian bigotry she is subjected to among her peers. Birdie finds that desire renders the space between whiteness and blackness intolerable, a condition that may arrest her own sexual maturation. She reflects,

> Maybe I would never be able to go all the way with a white boy. Sex was the only time, outside of the womb, when a person became one with another, when two people really melted together, into one body. Allowing a white boy inside of me would make my transformation complete, something I wasn't ready for. I thought about Stuart Langley. Just the week before, he had winked at me during an assembly in the school auditorium. Perhaps I would lose my virginity to him. At least he was black. But the thought of it depressed me. His high-pitched laughter got on my nerves. Besides, he seemed to have a thing for blonde girls. Maybe I would remain a virgin forever, never letting anything penetrate me.[33]

Senna's second novel, *Symptomatic*, invites readers to view it as a chronological follow-up to *Caucasia*, with a plot set in 1992 and an unnamed protagonist in her early twenties—a recent college graduate in her first professional job. The "Caucasia" of the earlier novel, the terrain of hegemonic American whiteness, is a metaphor for United States nation-building: constructed through xenophobia and insularity, demanding that Europeans assimilate through a deliberate ethnic cleansing ideally complete by the third generation. In the post–Civil Rights and pre–political correctness era of *Caucasia*, Americans like the New Hampshire teenagers express blatant racism with impunity, and blackness is routinely configured as a site of abjection. By the early 1990s, however, the urban unrest of the late 1960s and early 1970s had subsided—radical political groups such as the Black Panthers had been neutralized, and the ideology of multiculturalism provided

a veneer of racial tolerance through the celebration of diversity. A rein-
vigorated urban culture dominated by hip-hop music and dance[34] created
a social climate for a de-stigmatized consumption of black culture. In fact,
global capitalism facilitated cultural appropriation on a mass scale. This
new world constitutes the cultural terrain of *Symptomatic,* where characters from diverse ethnic backgrounds dabble in everything from hip-hop
to Buddhism with a sense of unflappable comfort and entitlement. Both
my mother and father, Senna writes in the protagonist's voice, "had wanted
a clean break . . . when they moved to California. They both believed in
ruptures and amnesia and had tried to instill in my brother and me a sense
of freedom from all tradition."[35]

Symptomatic features characters embodying the quintessentially American value of individualism and engaging in the characteristically American practice of personal reinvention. In this novel "passing" is less a strategy of survival than a performative mode, less a sign of resistance than an
indication of profound personal alienation, dislocation, and deracination.
The fact that the name of *Symptomatic*'s female narrator is never divulged
underscores the novel's bleak tone; there is little effort at any substantive
connection, either between the characters or between the book and the
reader. Senna has said she wrote *Symptomatic* with the noir genre in mind,
and the novel reads like a contemporary suspense thriller.

With its focus on a friendship between two women, one of whom
becomes obsessed with the other, *Symptomatic* bears a strong resemblance
to films such as Barbet Schroeder's *Single White Female* (1992). As in that
film, the mentally unstable character's relationship to her friend begins as
a fantasy of merging with the other woman, eventually devolving into a
murderous attempt to displace her object of desire. Greta, the obsessive
character of the novel, is in fact a creation—the alter ego of Vera, a marginal figure who dwells in a seedy underworld of drugs and prostitution,
regularly changing her identity to avoid creditors. As in Schroeder's film,
much of the action takes place in Vera's apartment, where the narrator is
living under the impression that she has sublet the space through Greta.
And as in *Single White Female,* the novel's climax involves a violent confrontation and ends with the unstable character Vera/Greta's death.

Symptomatic's two black/white women represent very different generations of mixed-race people. Greta is the post–World War II child of a German woman and a black American GI. Born in the 1950s; she is part of

a dispersed mixed-race group that grew up in isolation, imagining "that somewhere out there was a girl just like me . . . ."[36] Describing herself as "from Nowhere, Everywhere" she embodies the "marginal man," an ethnographic category created to describe, among others, mixed-race populations.[37] Greta's social-class background is ambiguous—working-class by virtue of being the child of an African American army soldier, yet also cosmopolitan through her German mother and a childhood spent traveling the globe. Yet Greta's cosmopolitanism does not broaden her cultural world; rather, she possesses the hermetic sensibility of many Americans who travel abroad through the military. The military labors to create bases that, to the extent that it is possible, are outposts of the United States, providing familiar food, consumer products, and media. The culture of the bases, however, is characterized by displacement and distance from the empire—incomplete and always slightly out of sync. Rather than expanding her world, Greta's military background has rendered her a woman stuck in a time capsule, culturally marked by outdated and somewhat vulgar tastes. Although she lives and works in New York City she has none of the flair associated with the urban setting. She wears "a color scheme from another era . . . [s]lashes of pink blush, pearlescent coral lipstick. Her eyes [are] decorated with sparkly blue eye shadow"[38] and she is partial to Houlihan's, a lowbrow chain restaurant that serves half-price hot wings during Happy Hour.

As a member of the post-*Loving*, biracial baby boom generation, *Symptomatic*'s narrator has the educated, socially progressive parents associated with "the golden love child" of the post–Civil Rights era—a white mother and black father who encourage their children to explore a freedom prioritizing personal fulfillment. Although her family is puzzled by the narrator's decision to move from the California Bay Area to work at a mainstream New York magazine, and at her taste for Wasp-y men, they do not attempt to influence her decisions. In New York, other characters interpret the narrator's Ivy League pedigree and her position as a writing fellow (at the magazine where Greta also works) as indications of privileged class status and thus "upscale" tastes. As different as the two women are, they share the same virtually white appearance enabling them to pass among white people, and rendering them unintelligible as black to many African Americans. Unlike Birdie in *Caucasia*, they have no need to invent ethnic identities explaining their looks: "the same straight brown hair and olive skin, and the same vague look about our features."[39] They blend

easily in the cosmopolitan mecca of urban New York. In the protagonist's
Bay Area home, the 1980s and 1990s were characterized by the increasing
demographic presence of interracial families and their integration into the
social life of the community. As Cole encourages Birdie to attend Berkeley
High School at the end of *Caucasia* she comments, "If you ever thought
you were the only one get ready. We're a dime a dozen out here."[40] Ten
years later, as the narrator in *Symptomatic* and her friends hang out in a
dorm room at an institution clearly meant to evoke Stanford University,
one jokes, "Mulattos these days are all ordinary and well adjusted. Even a
little boring [. . .] almost makes you miss the old head cases."[41]

Yet *Symptomatic*'s black/white women are "head cases" in their own
ways—one by virtue of mental illness and the other as a function of sheer
exhaustion over dealing with the question of racial intelligibility. The privileges of virtual whiteness do not insulate the narrator from having to
repeatedly negotiate whether, how, and when to reveal her blackness to
others. Like Birdie's, her face and body hide the evidence of racial difference in such a way that her claims to blackness are denied authority. The
questioning tone shaping Birdie's declaration at the Nkrumah School:
"Black is beautiful?" captures the uncertainty haunting African Americans who are not black enough. As the woman in *Symptomatic* reflects:
"'Who are you?' I didn't say anything. I just stared at him in the dark for
a moment, thinking of all the different answers to this question I had
already given. You know how it goes. The disclosure, followed by the edify-
ing speech. My body, the lesson."[42]

Whereas *Symptomatic*'s narrator is blind-sided by the racism of her white
lover's friends, she is generally anxious around African Americans, perpetually anticipating rejection. Her uneasy relationship with black characters
is often a function of their response to how she expresses—or does not
express—a racialized identity. A conversation between Flo, Vera's apartment
house neighbor, and the narrator brings this tension into full relief:

> "You black?" she repeated, chewing her gum and eyeing
> me up and down. "Corky and me made a bet. She thinks
> you're a sister."
> "Well," I said. "I am."
> "Hmmph," she said. "You sure got a white way of show-
> ing it."
> "Yeah, um," my words petered out. I'd heard this kind

of dig so many times before and it always stung me as if
it were for the first time.

"I'm just playin'," she said, smiling now with her mouth.
Her eyes remained dull and suspicious. "Want to come to
a Kwanzaa party? I'm on the planning committee."[43]

Their conversation echoes an anecdote related by Adrian Piper: "As an
undergraduate in the late 1960s and early 1970s, I attended an urban university to which I walked daily through a primarily black working-class
neighborhood. Once a black teenaged youth called to me, 'Hey white girl!
Give me a quarter!' I was feeling strong that day, so I retorted, 'I'm not
white and I don't have a quarter!' He answered skeptically, 'You sure look
white! You sure act white!'"[44]

Generally African Americans have a heightened awareness about racial
ambiguity and are more familiar with the wide variety of skin colors and
racialized features that exist among those who identify as black. Still, as
Adrian Piper insists, the idea that black people possess a kind of "racial
radar" enabling them to detect who is black is a myth. Behavior, particularly mutual acknowledgment between strangers, is the standard for how
African Americans communicate racial identity. Those capable of passing
are expected to convey their race to fellow blacks. The failure to purpose-
fully make this effort to connect runs counter to a long-standing norm
of behavior among African Americans to recognize others in the racial
group as kin. Virtually white women of the late twentieth century are in
a bind, risking rejection from those who judge them "not black enough."
However, as the one-drop rule encompasses people regardless of appearance, declining to engage in the ritual of mutual recognition is indeed
tantamount to "having a white way of showing" one's blackness or "acting white." Related to the Du Boisian notions of double consciousness
and the veil, mutual recognition, whether fleeting or more substantive,
is a respite from running the racist gauntlet of everyday life: a subtle but
fundamental way in which African Americans resist the dehumanizing
experience of circulating in mainstream society. "Can I ask you a question?" Senna has one character say. ". . . Are you a quadroon? . . . You must
be one of those 'new people' I keep reading about in the papers."[45]

Normative heterosexuality plays a powerful role in the way women are
constituted in the field of vision, their racial intelligibility overdetermined
by patriarchal entitlement. At one point in the novel the protagonist,

accompanied by a black male friend, encounters her ex-boyfriend on a street in the East Village. Although Andrew may be said to see her, she does not register as his ex-lover, the white woman he assumed she was. Her racially inflected sexuality is an aspect of her interactions with the three male lovers depicted in *Symptomatic*. For the WASP Andrew she is a persistent mystery; her dark looks compelled him to ask her, when they first met, if she spoke Spanish. Although her college liaison Claude appreciates her "black" backside, to him, she seems headed for a conventionally hip (and implicitly white) heteronormative lifestyle. Her lover Ivers, whom the reader learns the most about, has an ironic take on the figure of the mulatto/a, as his words above indicate—a teasing condescension aimed not so much at her as at the very idea of "new (biracial) people" transforming the tragic mulatto/a in United States culture.

The idea of the mulatto/a as emblematic of a "new people" preoccupies Greta; her obsessive desire for the narrator is shaped by the fantasy that together they will create a raceless paradise. The symptom to which the novel's title refers is an affliction embodied by both women, and brought on by what Senna implies is the dead end of late-1990s attempts to articulate a coherent notion of both identities and a social movement predicated on mixed race. Whereas Greta's descent into mental illness makes her an unambiguous casualty, the mulatto/a narrator's oscillation between passivity and paralysis is harder to read. She resembles the post–Civil Rights version of the tragic mulatto/a figure, immobilized between two worlds, perpetually a victim in both. It is also possible to discern a strategy in this black/ white woman's refusal to self-consciously proclaim a racialized identity. The way she moves through the world suggests that individualism guides her decisions. From the first academic publications to engage multiracial identity, mixed-race discourse has consistently emphasized the primacy of individual rights, a perspective summarized in a "Bill of Rights for Racially Mixed People" described by its author as resistant, revolutionary, and transformative.[46]

> I have the right:
> not to justify my existence in the world.
> not to keep the races separate within me.
> not to be responsible for people's discomfort with my
>   physical ambiguity.
> not to justify my ethnic legitimacy.

> I have the right:
> to identify myself differently than strangers expect me
>   to identify.
> to identify myself differently than how my parents
>   identify me.
> to identify myself differently than my brothers and
>   sisters.
> to identify myself differently in different situations.
> I have the right:
> to create a vocabulary to communicate about being
>   multiracial.
> to change my identity over my lifetime—and more
>   than once.
> to have loyalties and identify with more than one group
>   of people.
> to freely choose whom I befriend and love.

This Bill of Rights is clearly modeled on the profound ideological invest-ment in individual freedoms defining American liberal democracy. That value is what makes the multiracial identity movement such a vividly suc-cessful crossover phenomenon with white mainstream society; its demands on behalf of the individual are the inverse of traditional demands for social justice articulated by racialized groups. Advocates for multiracial interests have attempted to craft a successful argument that people of mixed race suffer discrimination when they are denied the ability to assert their per-sonal identity in scenarios requiring racial classification. Although such demands have made some difference in terms of how personal information is solicited—examples include Census 2000—the notion of mixed-race rights proves difficult to incorporate into public policy. Likewise, legal cases regarding mixed-race people and civil rights violations are rare. In fact, the mixed-race movement was often co-opted by public figures spearhead-ing the late twentieth century's successful efforts to dismantle affirmative action, a notable example being Ward Connerly (author of Proposition 209). Connerly has mobilized examples of mixed-race people who encounter obstacles based on their heritage or identity to buttress the notion that racial classification is inherently discriminatory.

Consistent with the African American community's incorporation of the one-drop rule, the NAACP is the most vociferous critic of any institutional recognition of mixed-race identity that would reduce the official population of black Americans. Yet mixed race is little more than a straw man, since only a small percentage of African Americans check more than one race. That Americans could check more than one race starting with the 2000 national census did not reduce the number of blacks (or any other racial group); the bureau of the census included people checking black in the African American group and noted their presence among those checking more than one category. This institutional practice is telling recognition of the ongoing problem of racial inequality, an acknowledgment of unfair treatment according to race, and implicitly the suggestion that people of mixed race experience racial discrimination.

Adrian Piper suggests for the subject inhabiting the space between black and white, "passing for black"—having one's racial authenticity interrogated by African Americans and being accused of being opportunistic by whites—is eminently more survivable than the inverse practice. The definition of whiteness as racially unmarked, and of blackness as determined by the one-drop rule, makes "passing for white" impossible without a complete disavowal of blackness.

> But the truth in my professors' accusations was that I had, in fact, resisted my parents' suggestion that, just this once, for admission to this most prestigious of graduate programs, I decline to identify my racial classification on the graduate admissions application, so that it could be said with certainty that I'd been admitted on the basis of merit alone. "But that would be passing," I protested. Although both my parents had watched many of their relatives disappear permanently into the white community, passing for white was unthinkable within the branches of my father's and mother's families to which I belonged. That would have been a really, authentically shameful thing to do.[47]

Multiracial activists base their logic on biracial peoples' experience, arguing that a person with one white and one black parent is passing if they identify as either white or black rather than both. Moreover, they claim the disavowal of one's white or black heritage is equally problematic—heritage being equated with an individual parent. However, being socialized as white goes far beyond the personal relationship one has with a white parent.[48] One of the most vexing aspects of the racial culture of the United States is the implicit equation between whiteness and the status of being fully human. The white subject's "unraced" privilege radically blinds him/her to the humanity of racialized subjects; they are reduced to stereotype and phantasm. In John Howard Griffin's seminal experiment of changing his skin color and passing as a black man in the South in 1959, he came to a profound awareness of the extent to which blindness and misperception structure the white American psyche. He writes at one point, "In the flood of light against white tile, the face and shoulders of a stranger—a fierce, bald, very dark Negro—glared at me from the glass. He in no way resembled me."[49] In effect, Griffin had been taught to *think white* rather than to *be human,* to perceive the stereotypes rather than to see another human being.[50]

Caucasia and *Symptomatic* expose the heavy price exacted for the unraced individualism of whiteness. But, just as Birdie cannot remember to forget that she is black, she is not so easily free of Jesse—a not quite white girl. How will Birdie move through this state of fragmentation? And what is on the other side?

In *Caucasia,* Senna's conclusion suggests a new possibility. Birdie's glimpse of a girl on a school bus brings the novel back to the first chapter, entitled "Face." This time the face is not Cole's. "One face toward the back of the bus caught my eye, and I halted in my tracks, catching my breath. It was a cinnamon-skinned girl with her hair in braids. She was black like me, a mixed girl . . . Then the bus lunched forward, and the face was gone with it, just a blur of yellow and black in motion."[51]

Caucasia's last image, "a blur of yellow and black in motion," speaks to the mobility of black/white women. This statement about movement is apt for the unnamed narrator of *Symptomatic,* a subject without a stable position on the identity continuum. *Symptomatic* also concludes with characters in motion, a comfortable modality for the unmoored people of the novel. The narrator remains haunted by Greta/Vera, the dual subject intent on creating a race-free utopia, virgin territory for the ambiguous, and free of the imperative to identify and the vulnerability inherent in identification. As the novel concludes, the protagonist has moved to southern California, finding a landscape in which displacement is a group norm, an experience shared by a critical mass and thus not characterized by the isolation precipitating Vera's descent into madness. This terrain is the precise inverse of a raceless fantasyland. Rather, the Los Angeles of *Symptomatic* is a cacophony of subjectivities both rooted and in motion, making provisional stops along an identity continuum that knows no beginning or end, but contains the potential for an infinitude of possibilities for affiliation and belonging.

CHAPTER 4

Faking the Funk? Mariah Carey, Alicia Keys, and the Politics of Passing

Mariah Carey and Alicia Keys are ideal figures through which to consider the post–Civil Rights era's apparent rehabilitation and transformation of the mulatto/a into a biracial subject of representation. Representations of these women indicate the mulatto/a has not been displaced. Rather, s/he embodies a racialized dichotomy that has morphed to accommodate new historical conditions. The compelling rise of black popular culture in the 1980s and 1990s virtually inverted the racial imperative that historically confronted the mulatto/a. Whereas the socioeconomic advantages of whiteness have not changed dramatically, blackness as cultural capital has achieved a status of desirability that, though comparable to its position in periods such as the Jazz Age, has an unprecedented reach, nationally and globally. In this context, black/white women have been at the center of many recent debates about black racial authenticity. This phenomenon opens up a space for a critical and theoretical reassessment of the relationship between the aesthetics of race and the aesthetics of nation during the past two decades.

Selected 1990s discourses about black/white women expressed echoes of hybrid vigor and degeneracy. Hybrid vigor was reflected in ideas about black/white women's singular beauty, and hybrid degeneracy in representations of them as emotionally fragile. Needless to say, both physical beauty and psychological vulnerability are hallmark traits of the tragic mulatto. Halle Berry's beauty is a late twentieth-century truism—so much so that the scientific journal *Nature* reports evidence of a "Halle Berry gene" suggesting a universal response to her image. Equations of mixed race with feminine beauty are clearly related to pseudoscientific notions of race as biology. Contemporary media echoed hybrid degeneracy in depictions of black/white women as emotionally vulnerable, prone to psychological instability, and being victimized in personal relationships, one example being Mariah Carey's highly publicized "breakdown" of 2001.

Representations of Mariah Carey and Alicia Keys reveal the struggle between hybridity and authenticity, a tension endemic to what makes a black icon a successful object of desire. I look at depictions of Carey and Keys in selected media aimed at African American audiences and consumers of black popular culture, as well as how they are depicted in print and visual broadcasts aimed at a general audience. The dualism inherent in the notion of the biracial hybrid both troubles the ways in which distinctions are made between groups and has the potential to undermine the stable sense of identity within a group. While the hybrid is a sign of difference, he/she is also a reminder that the races are not successfully segregated and there are not always clear physical distinctions between them. Whereas the hybrid may move with relative ease across boundaries and up hierarchies, he/she is also marginalized for being fragmented and multiple. The hybrid occupies a complex node of privilege and stigma in the American racial imaginary.

Just as the mulatto character in American literature has been "a vehicle for an exploration of the relationship between the races and, at the same time, an expression of the relationship between the races,"[1] contemporary images of black/white women enact similar relational dynamics between the races. In the late twentieth century, this symbolic function was complicated by the ways in which representations of mixed race increasingly reflected the commodification of interracial sex—or, the marketing of miscegenation. Black/white women such as Carey and Keys are not only the embodied result of sex between the races but are also symbolic fetish objects from more than one point of view: for white males intrigued by the idea of sex with a woman who is racially taboo but not so different from a white woman, for black males intrigued by the idea of sex with a woman who approximates the physical aesthetic of whiteness that is the feminine beauty ideal. Carey and Keys are figures that help to illuminate how the marketing of hybrid bodies as popular cultural icons becomes synonymous with the commodification of miscegenation—a conceptual negotiation of racial difference through sexual desire. The metaphor of race mixing, implying miscegenation and heterosexuality, operationalizes the inherent conflict between the taboo against interracial sex and the imperative to normative heterosexuality. The racially mixed female body becomes symbolic of both illicit sex and the incitement to an apparently transgressive heterosexuality, quickly recuperated and normalized through processes of desire, spectacle, and commodity. As icons of racialized and sexual desire Mariah Carey and Alicia Keys embody these dynamics in ways analogous to Halle Berry. Carey and Keys are powerful examples of how multiracial celebrities in the post–Civil Rights era enable the consumption of black popular culture without sacrificing the appeal of a "not quite white" female body.[2]

As post–Civil Rights era "rainbow babies," Mariah Carey and Alicia Keys are of a time when multiracial identities are part of America's social and cultural landscape. By the same token, popular cultural representations of black/white women emphasize a hypersexual image; a stereotype conflating mixed-race people with the taboo interracial sexuality that brought them into being.[3] For contemporary black/white women, the mulatta-as-whore image is also an enduring archetype.[4] Life parallels between Mariah Carey and Alicia Keys (along with Halle Berry) include being raised by single white mothers and the experience of absent black fathers. Both Carey and Keys became world-famous and won Best New Artist Grammy Awards on the strength of their debut albums—Carey in 1990 and Keys in 2001. The decade of difference here is a crucial factor in how the two women's careers diverge, with regard to how they have been marketed and to the tenor of media discourse about them. I begin by exploring the very public excoriation of Carey that accelerated following the terrorist attacks on the United States of September 11, 2001, moving on to a more explicit comparison of how representations of Carey and Keys engage in popular cultural discourses of "blackness."

"Is Mariah Carey exhausted, or just tired?" So began the African American music magazine *Vibe*'s "20 Questions" in the November 2001 issue, a monthly list of sardonic non sequiturs dishing the latest celebrity gossip. The dig referencing Carey's high-profile collapse and hospitalization at the end of summer 2001 also described a low point in her illustrious career.[5] Carey's feature film and star vehicle *Glitter*, a rags-to-riches tale of a biracial singer who becomes fabulously successful in 1980s New York, had spectacularly unfortunate timing, scheduled to open on September 11. The film's subsequent delayed debut was followed by an abysmal performance at the box office, along with disappointing sales for the film sound track.[6] Carey's famous voice sounded weak and under-rehearsed at the first benefit concert for victims of the terrorist attacks, recorded on sound stages without audiences and broadcast less than two weeks after September 11. Her vulnerability seemed evident when at one point she actually turned to her back-up singers to provide the powerfully sustained notes that are her trademark.

At some point most celebrities participate in regrettable projects, and the public delights in raking them over the coals when stars stumble in this fashion. In the weeks following September 11, however, the failure of *Glitter* became a running joke—and Mariah Carey a safe target for a media jittery about content. The referent seemed ubiquitous and lasted for weeks: a *Saturday Night Live* parody of a news broadcast announcing the Bush administration's search for Osama bin Laden in remote, unpopulated places—thus every movie theater playing *Glitter*.[7] The actor Billy Crystal's deadpan at another benefit concert: "Regardless of our differences, we can all come together as Christians, Jews, Muslims, Buddhists—and agree that Mariah Carey should never make another movie." In fall 2001, *Glitter* became the metaphor marking particularly humiliating failures.

In the years following *Glitter*, Halle Berry and Jennifer Lopez had similarly humiliating film experiences. Like *Glitter*, Lopez's *Gigli* (2003) and Berry's *Catwoman* (2004) were high-profile features, strongly marketed and released with significant fanfare. Critics were wary of the pairing of then real-life lovers Lopez and Ben Affleck in the comedy-crime caper *Gigli*. Although Lopez always acts with infectious charm, the couple, separated soon after the film was released, had no on-screen chemistry. *Catwoman* seemed to have far greater potential. Following on the heels of *Monster's Ball* and in the venerable and sexy footsteps of Eartha Kitt and Michelle Pfeiffer, the action-adventure was potentially an ideal star vehicle. The media preceding the film showcased Berry in her character's sexy dominatrix-style costumes. Like *Glitter* and *Gigli*, *Catwoman* proved a huge disappointment. All three films received multiple "Razzie" nominations. The Razzies are a twenty-five-year institution in Los Ange-les—they bestow tongue-in-cheek awards (dis)honoring the worst of film in a given year. Mariah Carey, Jennifer Lopez, and Halle Berry all won Worst Actress awards, and both *Gigli* and *Catwoman* won worst on-screen couple and worst film.[8]

What makes *Glitter* different from *Gigli* or *Catwoman*? Carey's film is quasi-autobiographical—the protagonist is a singer discovered in the 1980s club scene of New York. She is biracial and from an underprivileged background. The film knowingly satirizes the way show business exploits racial ambiguity. In a scene depicting Carey filming a music video, the director exclaims: "We ask ourselves, is she black? Is she white? We don't care. She's exotic. I want to see more of her breasts." As fleeting as such moments of insight may be, they demonstrate Carey's reflexivity about her own position in the business in which she has been so successful.

Why did the failure of Carey's film provoke so much gleeful scorn, and why did it constitute a point of reference in popular culture's postmor-tem period of recovery following September 11? Danzy Senna's *Caucasia* invoked the metaphor "canaries in the coal mine" to describe the ways that mulatto/as act as barometers of social racism—in a climate poisoned by it, they die. Does Mariah Carey's status as an easy target at that point of crisis reflect our culture's generalized love/hate relationship with celebrities? Does a hybrid body, symbolic of racial ambiguity and ethnic multiplicity, pose a specific kind of threat when "the enemy" assumes no fixed body? In the multiple identity crisis that followed September 11, the incitement to rally around Carey's failed body (of work) points to a heightened hostility toward subject positions "marked by a border condition, a position at the rim . . . neither fully inside nor fully outside."[9]

At the beginning of Mariah Carey's career, a combination of factors rendered her racial identity opaque and as such inconsistently interpreted by the media. Undeniably, the way in which Sony Music orchestrated the launch of her career reflected the resources usually lavished on promising white artists.[10] Promotional materials that made no mention of Carey's racial heritage seemed to exploit her physical ambiguity. For some, the absence of explicit racial classification combined with aggressive market-ing made her whiteness a given. Thus in July 1990 the *Los Angeles Times* called her a "white soulster . . . poised to give the British singer Lisa Stans-field a run for her money."[11] Eight months later in a review of Carey's first music video, the *Los Angeles Times* had not changed its reporting of Carey's racial classification, although a reviewer complained that the video gave no clues as to "how Carey, who is white, acquired such strong black-gospel roots and why she comes across so vividly as a product of the black culture."[12] In that same month, March 1991, *Ebony* magazine published a feature on Carey entitled "Not Another White Girl Trying to Sing Black."[13] In that interview Carey expressed that she was a biracially identified woman with mixed musical influences. The *Ebony* piece was subsequently hailed as Carey's "coming out" as a black woman and indicative of a belated effort to stop capitalizing on the racial ambiguity that her record label seemed intent on promoting.

In 1990, the year Carey's first album was released, and before her racial heritage had been made public, she appeared on two late-night talk shows—*Arsenio Hall* (canceled 1994, returning 2013) and *The Tonight Show* with Jay Leno.[14] There is a significant contrast in the content of the two programs because the African American television host Arsenio Hall was not permitted to interview the emerging star (although she performed twice on his show within three months). Is it possible that Sony feared Hall would "out" Mariah by exposing her black heritage? Jay Leno, it seems safe to say, was utterly clueless. Leno appeared smitten by Carey in a manner exceeding the usual flirtatious banter that characterizes conversation between male hosts and female guests. During a very funny interview in a documentary about Carey's career, the super-producer and musical duo Jimmy Jam and Terry Lewis deconstructed Leno's demeanor. The film cuts back and forth between footage of Leno's interview with Carey and the documentary commentary by Jam and Lewis:

> Leno: "You look like my wife when I met her."
>
> Jam & Lewis: "Jay was trying to get a date or something."
>
> Leno: "That's why I was staring at you."
>
> Jam & Lewis: "Jay was like, flabbergasted—he was like stumbling over words and stuff."
>
> Leno: "You have the same . . . twenty years distant . . . I mean you're very pretty."
>
> Jam & Lewis: "I thought Jay was gonna lose it."
>
> Leno: "I don't mean to embarrass you."

During the exchange, Carey responds like a typical twenty-one-year-old girl on the cusp of stardom: smiling somewhat nervously and tossing her hair. I contend that Leno's comment, "You look like my wife," indicates his ignorance of Carey's black heritage. Adrian Piper observes:

> No reflective and well-intentioned white person who is consciously concerned to end racism wants to admit instinctively recoiling at the thought of being identified as black herself. But if you want to see such a white person do this, just peer at the person's facial features and tell her, in a complementary tone of voice, that she looks as though she might have some black ancestry, and watch her reaction. It's not a test I or any black person finds particularly pleasant to apply . . . and having once done so inadvertently, I will never do it again.[15]

Rather, that Mariah Carey might look like Jay Leno's wife indicates the extent to which Carey's racial appearance exceeds a black/white paradigm. Her "look" at that point in her career—dark curly hair and deep-colored cosmetics—could be interpreted as stylistic markers for Latina, Jewish, and Leno's own Italian ethnicity. These same features would, subsequent to the *Ebony* article, be read as "black" and evidence of America's one-drop rule. As an Italian American, Leno is part of an ethnic group that has become "white," yet is subject to enduring racial myths, including the idea that Italy's proximity to Africa has permanently tainted that genetic pool.[16] His televised interview with Carey took place in southern California at a point in 1990 when awareness of multiracial identity was becoming increasingly common. Thus, the discourses of miscegenation and intergenerational desire that surface in the interview compete with other discourses about the unstable status of "whiteness" and monoracial classifications in general.

The collapse of these complex dynamics of ethnicity into the black/white paradigm however, facilitated the myth that Carey's critics and fans were allowed to believe that she was white, however briefly. Thus, the specter of racial passing has become a fixed aspect of her image, along with endless discussion of her ethnic identity and racial allegiances. Mariah Carey can pretend to be white before audiences to whom she looks white enough, but the one-drop rule always already renders any claim to whiteness—even an implicit, silent one—inauthentic. Although there was no consensus among black journalists and music fans about Carey's ethnic heritage when her first album was released, some maintained that contrary to what was being reported in the mainstream press she wasn't "just" white. Rather than being publicly outed however, Carey and Sony were able to orchestrate the terms of the revelation about her heritage, which the black press then led the way in reporting. The pleasure of gossiping about celebrities who "pass" is a recurrent theme in ethnic communities, a phenomenon that may become conflated with an imperative for complicity that has deep historical resonance for African Americans. As anachronistic as racial passing might seem, in late 2001 the television talk show hosted by Ananda Lewis featured the dilemma experienced by black people whose relatives have passed as white.[17] On one hand, the 1990s tendency for celebrities to emphasize multiracial identity is less likely to engender resentment among contemporary black audiences who understand market forces: if multiculturalism is in, claiming mixed identity may not be about rejecting one's blackness, but about getting paid.[18] The apparently deliberate marketing of Carey's racial ambiguity illuminates the complex stakes at play in a popular music world in which the ability to "cross over"—with regard to both musical genres and racial boundaries—is extremely lucrative. Regardless of Sony's intentions, by marketing her as they did, the record label capitalized on the multiracial/multicultural vogue gaining momentum since the 1980s.[19]

The media's virtually universal derision of Carey following September 11 coincided with the emergence of Alicia Keys, who gave an electrifying performance in one of her first nationally televised appearances at the same post-9/11 benefit concert that featured a below-par Carey. Overall, Keys's career has been characterized by a marketing strategy that fixes her firmly in the realm of black celebrity despite her ambiguous look and biracial heritage. Whereas Carey has been marketed in the pop category which is coded white, Keys's music is classified in a black idiom, part of the late 1990s/early millennial neo-soul r&b movement typified by solo artists such as Erykah Badu, Angie Stone, India.arie, and D'Angelo. As such, Alicia Keys benefits from flattering comparisons to artists like Mariah Carey because of the way in which musical styles are rendered as binary and racialized opposites. While pop is a style that through its virtue as a mainstream form becomes classified as "white," which comes with undeniable privileges, it is also represented as a paradigmatic model of illegitimacy when compared to black urban music forms, which are equated with authenticity. Pop is associated with commercialism and superficiality, and pop artists and their audiences, especially when they are female, are stereotyped as being controlled, manipulated, and duped.[20] Such distinctions are meaningful for media and contemporary audiences well versed in the notion that "blackness" constitutes the currency, the vernacular, and the standard not only for "realness" but also for what constitutes the artistic cutting edge.

Although Mariah Carey's collaborations with black songwriters, musicians, and producers dates from the beginning of her career and she has consistently worked in black musical idioms such as gospel and rhythm and blues, it was only when she began collaborating with rappers and hip-hop artists (on the 1997 album *Butterfly*) that her involvement in a black-identified musical idiom became newsworthy. The perception that Carey's involvement with black music and artists is "new" was expressed through reactions that ranged from skepticism to outright hostility from white and black audiences alike. In July 2000 an Internet site reported that the single from *Rainbow* (an album released in 1999) was a chart flop. The site warned, "Her forays into hip hop and r&b, and her work with "urban producers" may be alienating top 40 listeners." The change in Carey's music, along with her separation from Tommy Mottola—who signed her to Sony—after a five-year marriage, seemed to accelerate her emergence as a black female celebrity. Since her 1998 divorce, she has made appearances at the NAACP Image Awards, pursued high-profile collaborations with African American superstars such as the late Whitney Houston, and been linked romantically with a number of prominent black men (including the baseball star Derek Jeter, another biracial celebrity). In addition, Carey's image on magazine covers and in music videos became significantly more sexual, with copy that repeatedly alluded to her desirability.

The odd double standard implicit in the metaphor of racial passing involves the idea that passing is a unidirectional gesture; "passing for black" is not logical because of the one-drop rule.[21] Yet the imperative for racial authenticity, along with the contradictory impulses of black pride and the internalization of racism, makes Carey a target precisely because her physical ambiguity and cultural hybridity trouble her claim to black identity. The Jewish-American actress Sandra Bernhard, a performer

known for ironic explorations of racial mimicry and masquerade, makes
Carey's racial identity a frequent target of ridicule precisely in this regard.
Throughout her own career, Bernhard has made blackness a touchstone
for her explorations of difference. Early on, she was known for the comment, "Have you ever seen lips like this on a white woman?" here deploying blackness to make herself white, rather than Jewish.

Bernhard commented on Carey's mixed racial heritage and her sexuality to pointed effect in her one-woman show *I'm Still Here . . . Damn It!*
Published excerpts of Bernhard's comments include: "Now [Mariah's]
trying to backtrack on our asses, gettin' real niggerish up there at the
Royalton Hotel suite, with Puff Daddy and all the greasy chain-wearing
Black men. 'Oooh, Daddy . . . I got a little bit of Black in me, too. I didn't
tell you that?'"[22] Here Bernhard mimics Black English, enacting a self-
authorizing to invoke stereotypes of black men and mulatto/a sexuality as
a way to "out" Carey as a person intent on exploiting black identity.

In a May 1999 interview with *Mirabella* magazine, Carey herself offered
commentary on Bernhard's monologue:

> Sandra Bernhard used words that every African Ameri-
> can I know—and definitely I, personally, find inappro-
> priate. *If my skin were two shades darker, she wouldn't have
> done it* [my emphasis].
>
> [C]alling me a "phony white bitch" and saying I was
> "acting niggerish" is acceptable because she figures,
> "Who's gonna stick up for her?" . . . And yeah I'm a freak-
> ing mutt, I'm a triracial freak, but she implied I was a
> white person trying to be black. And it's offensive to me,
> because I've been a victim of racism on both sides.[23]

Carey is astutely aware of the ways that her "white-looking" features can
be read as defusing Bernhard's racial slurs. And her question, "Who's gonna stick up for her?" goes to the heart of her liminal position. The vitriol
that fuels Bernhard's mockery of Carey is reminiscent of Adrian Piper's
experience of the hostility directed toward her by white people who are
inexplicably furious when they discover that, despite "visual evidence" to
the contrary, Piper is African American. She writes,

> Once exposed as a fraud of this kind, you can never

regain your legitimacy. For the violated criterion of legitimacy implicitly presumes an absolute incompatibility between the person you appeared to be and the person you are now revealed to be, and no fraud has the authority to convince her accusers that they merely imagine an incompatibility where there is none in fact. The devaluation of status consequent on such exposure is, then, absolute, and the suspicion of fraudulence spreads to all areas of interaction.[24]

Carey's statement "I've been a victim of racism on both sides," evokes the character Birdie's experience in *Caucasia:* the discovery that African Americans, like whites, police the ambiguous boundaries of race and reject those who do not meet the community's standard of racial authenticity. Adrian Piper deconstructs the hostility reserved for blacks judged "not black enough" as having given her unexpected insight "into the way whites feel when they are made the circumstantial target of blacks' justified and deep-seated anger . . . because the anger is justified, one instinctively feels guilty. But because the target is circumstantial and sometimes arbitrary, one's sense of fairness is violated. One feels both unjustly accused or harassed, and also remorseful and ashamed at having been the sort of person who could have provoked the accusation."[25]

Carey's question, "Who's gonna stick up for her?" particularly evokes the dilemma of light-skin privilege for women, who, when they become "representative" of black women, are implicated in the racist standards of beauty that make them icons. Carey's remarks seem to indicate her awareness of the dearth of empathy that attends being an oppressive symbol to the women whom Alice Walker has called "black black women."[26] And yet, Mariah Carey and Tiger Woods, two of the new "mulatto" celebrities that emerged in the 1990s, embody precisely the kind of racial multiplicity that belies the conventional racial binary. In Carey's case, Latina ethnicity emerges repeatedly to challenge the tendency to place her on one side of the black/white opposition. She has been featured on the cover of *Latina* magazine and is included in a volume in the series *Famous People of Hispanic Heritage.* In another era Carey might have attempted to deploy Latina identity to escape the stigma of blackness as Philippa Schuyler attempted with Felipa Monterro. In the contemporary United States, however, hip-hop culture includes numerous Latino groups and stylistic and linguistic elements as well as celebrity icons such as Jennifer Lopez, who is representative of both hip-hop culture and the "Latino explosion" of the late 1990s. Apparently, it is also the case that Carey has had a high profile in Spanish-language media, particularly when she was romantically involved with the Latin pop superstar Luis Miguel.[27]

Mariah Carey's style can signify as black, white, or Latina, yet over the years her skin becomes more porcelain, her hair increasingly blonde. We could almost say that the "blacker" she gets, the "whiter" she looks, a factor that in her case derives significantly from the way that her hair is styled—"bone straight" as African American stylists say, and platinum blonde. In August 2001 the tabloid magazine *Star* ran a feature of "before" and "after" photographs of celebrities, contrasting images from early in their careers with contemporary shots. The "before" photograph of Carey depicted her with the dark curly hairstyle she wore in her Leno interview. Of this look *Star* wrote, "Mariah Carey had a voice like a songbird and hair like a bird's nest when her first album . . . debuted in 1990. The 20-year-old scored four hits off the album—but it wasn't until she went from shaggy to sleek sex bomb that she truly conquered the world."[28]

This kind of de-racializing process—hair that becomes straighter and blonder, bodies photographed so that skin appears lighter, the use of pastel rather than deep-toned cosmetics—seems to be an unfortunate by-product of fame for many female celebrities (including those classified as "white"). Radical transitions are evident in a dramatically short period of time, as Jennifer Lopez went from a raven-haired "Butter Pecan Rican" in *Vibe* magazine in 1997 to a blonde-streaked "Diva Loca" on *Vibe*'s cover in 1999. The rapper Lil' Kim is one of the more extreme examples of the phenomenon, transforming from a fleshy, dark-haired, and chocolate-skinned vixen to a platinum blonde, gym-toned, surgically enhanced, and mahogany-hued creation in just one short year. Notwithstanding the importance of artifice in the transgressive aesthetics of hip-hop, these processes of lightening and Anglicization recall the ultra-white aesthetic developed for Hollywood film actresses of the 1950s.[29] As in the case of Dorothy Dandridge and Halle Berry, visually oriented cultural texts privilege a narrow range of racialized types.

Alicia Keys's style is consistent with the aesthetic popularized by neo-soul female artists such as Lauryn Hill, Erykah Badu, Angie Stone, Jill Scott, and India.arie. These women self-consciously embody "positive" representations of blackness that both derive from black cultural nationalist discourses and constitute a more contemporary feminist comment on the gendered aesthetic that dictates that the body become progressively thinner and lighter-skinned and the hair straighter with fame. That racialized political and social meanings tend to be inscribed on the bodies of female celebrities is linked to both the generalized Western cultural tendency to conflate appearance with femininity (as in John Berger's assertion that "men act, women appear"[30]) and a more distinctly African American struggle over the politics of appearance. Patricia Williams has written,

> Black women's hair anxiety has a lot of history, even a legal history. Legal theorist Paulette Caldwell has written about how black women have actually had to sue for the right to wear their hair naturally—i.e., unstraightened, kinky, liberated from chemical "enhancement"—without being fired from their employment. (My favorite case in that litany involved a woman who sued to be able to wear her hair in "cornrows," cornrowing being a traditional African style of braiding hair. Not only was she required to conform to her employer's demands, she was then chided for "imitating Bo Derek.")[31]

Mariah Carey and Alicia Keys—young, slender, light-skinned, and conventionally attractive—possess the hybrid bodies with the greatest potential to move across and beneath the color line, making ideal subjects for the type of molding female celebrities undergo. Despite their physical similarities, Alicia Keys's career has been managed to circumvent Mariah Carey's awkward transition from white to black, and recurrent whisper campaigns about her racial passing. Black signifiers were consistently and strategically deployed to market Keys's music and style. Early in her career, she appeared on the cover of several magazines aimed at black women, including *Essence* (March 2002) and *Today's Black Woman* (October 2001), in the cornrows that have become her trademark.[32] Representations of Carey and Keys underscore Kobena Mercer's contention that hair is "the

most tangible sign of racial difference," and particular textures and colors occurring "naturally" intersect with questions of political and social value.[33] Two covers from the African American music magazine *Vibe* feature particularly striking images deploying hair among other signifiers. In November 1998 Carey appeared in a silver lamé bikini, her hair styled in wavy, blonde-streaked tresses. The caption declares: "Mariah breaks it down! Miss Carey busts loose on Whitney, Derek Jeter, love and lust and mixed-race melodrama." In September 2002, Alicia Keys appeared on the cover of *Vibe*'s annual "Juice" issue, which features that year's most successful and interesting artists. Keys wears black jeans emblazoned with a black power salute, a halo-like Afro framing her cornrows. Keys's skin appears to be browner than in earlier magazine covers and her hair looks black rather than brown. She seems altogether darker than on the covers of *Essence* in March 2002, and *Today's Black Woman* in October 2001.[34] *Vibe*'s cover brings to mind the racialized aesthetic expressed just months earlier in May 2002, when Keys joined rapper Eve on the video for "Gangsta Love," the first single from *Eve-olution*.[35] Eve's skin color, a medium-brown shade, makes her significantly darker than Keys. In the video directed by Little X, lighting techniques render the women nearly identical in skin color. The darkening of Keys on the *Vibe* cover and the "Gangsta Love" video is a fascinating aesthetic counterpoint to phenomena such as *Time* magazine's infamous darkened cover photo of O. J. Simpson on June 27, 1994. Gender and marketing reframe the familiar association of darkness with stigma.

For many years Mariah Carey's collaborations with hip-hop artists of impeccable pedigree generated criticism and bolstered rather than diminished the ongoing whisper campaign that she was passing (as black). Music critics deplored the marketing strategy as alienating her core audience of pop (assumed white) fans and predicted it would fail to cross over to r&b (assumed black) consumers. This narrative demonstrates the resistance to acknowledging pop music's strong roots in r&b. Mariah Carey's compositions and performances express this continuity—a factor instigating the "confusion" about her racial identity in the first place. The music industry's resistance to substantive connections between these genres demonstrates the power of historical efforts to contain and deny that American music is a site of race mixing. Mariah Carey self-identifies as a mixed-race woman, and crosses musical boundaries that represent miscegenation. Alicia Keys is black-identified and performs intra-racial crossings, positions and moves that do not generate similar resistance.

Vibe's 1998 image of Carey with the reference to "mixed-race melodrama" was published at a moment when the question of a "multiracial" category on Census 2000 generated debate, and Americans of African descent reported in majority numbers that they were likely to check only the "black" category, regardless of whether they were of mixed descent.[36] In September 2002 *Vibe* did not draw attention to Alicia Keys's biracial heritage. It is tempting to place Mariah Carey on the "tragic mulatto" side and Alicia Keys on the "well-adjusted and black-identified mulatto" side of a racial identity binary, just as they are positioned at racialized ends of a musical binary. The realm of black celebrity and the ways that it intersects with the spectrum of ethnic identity and hierarchies of value, however, demands a more complex assessment of their iconic significance. In his brilliant comic strip *The Boondocks*, Aaron MacGruder regularly pilloried politically conservative African Americans during President George W. Bush's administrations. Along with then National Security adviser Condoleezza Rice, Mariah Carey appeared in a March 2002 strip as a nominee for "Most Embarrassing Black Person of the Year" (for her performance in *Glitter*, of course). In the strip's last frame McGruder's biracial character

Jazmine protests, "Hey! I liked *Glitter*!" McGruder's double gesture—a political critique of Carey's artistic choices and the empathetic representation of a young girl's desire to claim a "positive" role model—perfectly captures the "to and fro"[37] mode of analysis that the black/white woman in contemporary culture demands.

Alicia Keys's music has not undergone dramatic change in the course of her career. The rhythm and blues ballad remains her musical forte—plaintive love songs composed of a gorgeous aural entwinement of piano and voice. Keys's breakout hit "Fallin'" from her first album *Songs in A Minor* (2001) is lyrical simplicity personified—highlighting how composition and performance can infuse a generic love song with passion and presence. Music videos are the more compelling registers of Keys's development as an artist, activist, and celebrity. These visual works track one of the most important elements in marketing Keys as a "black" artist—the aesthetics of style. Four videos directed by Chris Robinson, two from *Songs in A Minor* and two from her 2007 album *As I Am*, make clear the essential role of visual representation and narrative in constructing Keys's racial iconicity. A fifth video (also directed by Chris Robinson) for the single "My Boo," from R&B superstar Usher's 2004 album *Confessions* features Keys in their Grammy award-winning duet. This video is an example of personal style articulating with cinematography and editing to produce Keys in a radically different mode of black femininity from prior incarnations. "My Boo" is an important transitional moment at the point of mid-career for this artist.

Popular culture theorist Mark Anthony Neal contends that part of Alicia Keys's allure for the critical mainstream is having been "blessed with "millennial exotic" good looks (read: light, bright, and racially ambiguous) [. . .]."[38] Undeniably, Keys's mixed-race beauty is a marketing advantage; making her appealing across the ethnic spectrum of audiences for r&b and soul music. Representations of Keys indicate what I take to be her own (and her management's) investment in being perceived as unambiguously African American. What are the stakes of constructing a biracial woman as "black," and how does one successfully perform this type of "passing"? Along with the factor of Keys's "millennial exotic" good looks, her education—classical music training and attendance at Columbia University (although she did not earn a degree) are routes to social mobility—advantages associated with biracial heritage, and rightly so.[39] By deemphasizing both the privileges and pitfalls of biracial identity, J Records' marketing apparatus and Keys's own self-representations in media minimized the possibility of being tagged with the mulatto/a label that long bedeviled Mariah Carey's career.

Alicia Keys's wardrobe in "Fallin'" and "A Woman's Worth"—tight leather pants, revealing tops and jaunty hats—expresses urban street chic, locating her solidly among her age peers who identify with hip-hop culture. As the definitive musical genre of hip-hop culture, rap occupies a critical node of identity. Keys's aesthetic in these early videos is the contemporary incarnation of the strikingly gender-neutral, far less conventionally feminine style distinctive of women artists during rap's "old school" period (the early 1980s to mid-1990s). Performers such as Queen Latifah, Salt-n-Pepa, and TLC wore the same oversized pants, overalls, shirts, and bandannas that male artists still wear today. Both onstage and off, gender-neutral style asserted parity with men in the musical idiom and in urban space. The 1990s was a golden age for women in rap and hip-hop. Subsequently, the uneven presence of women in rap seems related to the development of a sexier incarnation of women in hip-hop music. Retentions of the old school persist in "Fallin'" and "A Woman's Worth," where the protagonists are working-class street-savvy black women, and Keys punctuates her singing with the hip-hop body language deployed by male performers.

The video for "Fallin'" takes on one of the most urgent of issues for the urban underclass: incarceration. The economic turn to prisons as revenue-generating institutions is depicted through its intimate effects on individuals, relationships, and ethnic community.[40] As the protagonist, Alicia Keys rides on a bus filled with black women and children traveling the many miles separating state and federal prisons from cities for the opportunity to spend perhaps an hour with a husband, a boyfriend, the father of one's children. The video's transition to substantive critique occurs when the camera shifts the focus from women in love with prisoners to an oft-overlooked subject: the incarcerated woman of color. The heroine's lament: "I keep on fallin' in and out of love with you. I never loved someone the way that I love you," becomes a more layered comment on the politics of race, gender, and criminality.

The critical sequence supporting this reading occurs when the bus transporting Keys passes a field filled with women in orange prison jump-suits working under the supervision of white male guards brandishing nightsticks. "Fallin'" makes a rare acknowledgment of women of color accused and convicted of crimes.[41] The sheer numbers of black men in prison eclipses a grim statistic: black women, less than 10 percent of American women, account for 50 percent of the female prison popula-tion. As the bus approaches, the laboring women initially appear as spots of vivid color, the grid-like image of their bodies in rows conjuring a minimalist artistic composition. This depersonalized, passive image shifts dramatically when the women turn as one to gaze at the passing bus, taking up the song's refrain. The inclusion of women prisoners in "Fal-lin'" resists normative notions of race, gender, and criminality that render "all the blacks men."[42] The video challenges dominant cultural narratives making men de facto representations of the imprisoned black body. In this sense, incarceration is experienced collectively as a racialized condition. Subsequently, as the camera shifts to close-ups of women's faces, gender re-enters the field of vision to raise urgent questions about these prisoners. One is haunted by their expressions of numb resignation and deep despair. Clearly, they are bereft even of the fleeting comfort male prisoners experi-ence during brief visits with the women who love them.

"Fallin'" constructs the pain of loving a prisoner as a gendered condi-tion—women lose their men to a criminal justice system rife with extreme racial disparities in sentencing, and their attempts to stay in relationships with these men are physically and emotionally draining. The video's depic-tion of the women in the field enables "Fallin'" to raise the question of how incarcerated women fit the narrative's gendered construct. One very real possibility is the phenomenon of women as "collateral damage" in the drug war. Girlfriends unaware they are in possession of drugs are convicted of possession; grandmothers unaware or unable to prevent grandsons who are living with them from selling drugs are convicted of selling.[43] The representation of incarcerated women in "Fallin'" suggests the potentially dire consequences of "fallin' in and out of love." Loving a prisoner remains a gendered condition, and women with this problem dwell inside and outside the boundaries of the prison.

Released after "Fallin'," the video for "A Woman's Worth" features char-acters negotiating the quotidian challenge of how social-class mobility strains relationships among African Americans. With lyrics that articulate a more explicit position on gender relations, "A Woman's Worth" provides a more literal blueprint for the story told in the video. The lyrics address how intimacy between men and women is impacted when the fruits of middle-class status—objects of consumption—overdetermine the ways men express appreciation for the women in their lives. Keys's protagonist negotiates love with a man seeking middle-class employment. As he becomes increasingly frustrated, he begins to feel the strain between two types of masculinity: that represented by his "boys" hanging out on the corner, who mock his business attire, and the middle-class masculinity represented by professional employment. Keys's lyrics insist that while she is worth all the things he might buy for her, her true value—a woman's worth—cannot be captured by any of these objects.

> Wanna please wanna keep wanna treat your woman right
> Not just dough but to show that you
> Know she is worth your time
> You will lose if you choose to refuse to put her first
> She will if she can find a man who knows her worth.

This r&b ballad works against the grain of gender relations conveyed in many rap songs, where heterosexual desire is defined as a strikingly materialist mode of exchange: luxury goods for sex. Male performers continually boast of their ability to provide brand-name objects to attract desirable women. Interestingly, the analogue of such songs critiques these same women for their materialism—branding them "gold diggers."[44] The anti-materialist perspective in "A Woman's Worth" is an example of how Keys is in conversation with rap music's troubling representations of gender relations. Despite women's marginalization in rap music, hip-hop culture gives them a way to engage this male-dominated territory through soul, pop, and r&b.[45]

In the music video for "My Boo" Alicia Keys's image morphed from a "raw unabashedly street persona"[46] to a hyper-feminine type one rarely witnesses in her live performances. Her familiarity with director Chris Robinson may account for her willingness to portray such a dramatically different persona. Subsequent videos for songs from *As I Am* (also directed by Robinson) reflect this turn in gender representation. Depicting Keys in a less intensely glamorous fashion, they nonetheless resemble "My Boo" far more than the earlier videos. How is black women's agency affected by the transition to unequivocally feminine style? "My Boo" addresses this question in a compelling way by suggesting that economic equality between men and women corrects the tendency to interpret sexually provocative style as evidence of a woman exercising her only form of power.

Like many of Keys's own videos, "My Boo's" female protagonist is a version of Keys herself, in this case a star at the top of her game. Usher also plays a version of himself. He is a star, her peer, and her childhood crush. "My Boo" begins with a scene in a music video within the video: Usher sits on a bar counter surrounded by scantily clad, gyrating women. As the camera caresses long slim legs and zooms in on cleavage, Usher raps of being a pimp and a player. Watching the image from his living room, Usher turns off the video, lies down on a couch and begins singing the romantic ballad about first love. Alicia Keys sings her part of the duet in a lavish hotel suite, stretched out on a king-sized bed. In a slinky slip, her mane of "bone-straight" hair flowing across the bedspread, Keys resembles the "video vixens" of the opening scene. The song dwells on the pair's first kiss, and by the 2 minute 18 second mark of "My Boo," we have seen six extreme close-ups of Keys's lips. Are these shots objectifying? How do they differ from the erotic close-ups of Usher's video vixens? For the women in Usher's video within a video, beauty and sexual desirability are their primary currency. As in similar videos such as Outkast's "I Like the Way You Move," they are depicted as quasi-tribes of desirable female bodies reinforcing the sexual power of male artists. Because she is an artist in her own right, Keys's beauty and desirability are individual qualities rather than her primary currency.

"My Boo" deploys important class-related visual elements to suggest that gender plays a key role in how successful, wealthy African Americans negotiate racial authenticity. The video intercuts scenes of each character making their way to Times Square, where they meet and reconcile. Alicia Keys throws a fashionable trench coat over her lingerie, slips on stiletto heels, and takes a limousine. Usher, dressed in the black man's urban uniform of loose pants and "hoody," takes the subway and walks the street, on the way having a hostile moment with a cab driver when he crosses against the light. Although Usher is among black male artists who perform in tailored suits, his ability to move through public space suggests that authentic black masculinity requires maintaining a connection to the street. For women, moving away from the quasi-tomboy aesthetic of the street is a rite of passage. Numerous women in hip-hop undergo this morphing phenomenon: Queen Latifah, Salt-n-Pepa, Mary J. Blige, the late Aaliyah. Assuming a glamorous feminine aesthetic is less likely to imperil racial authenticity, or "realness," because this process works against the historical "un-gendering" of African American women.

For Alicia Keys, the transition to a conventional feminine aesthetic involves the risk of undermining her carefully constructed racial identity. A more ambiguous appearance brings her closer to embodying the black/white woman. This subject re-animates African Americans' ongoing struggle to reconcile the porous boundaries of blood and sex which continually threaten to destabilize black identity. The timing of "My Boo," released in late 2004, shortly preceded Keys's debut on the covers of mainstream women's magazines such as *Lucky* (February 2005) and *Seventeen* (April 2005)—where she appeared with straightened hair. Up to that point, Keys had been featured nearly exclusively on the covers of African American magazines, virtually always styled with her signature cornrows and braids. This move away from Afro-centric aesthetics indicates confidence that representations in print media successfully solidified her position as a black artist. Straight hair under these circumstances is a valid choice rather than a sign of "passing."

Unsurprisingly, subsequent images of Keys on magazine covers, along with her style in brief appearances on televised shows such as 2008's Academy Awards, are more glamorous than ever. (At the Oscars Keys resembled Rita Hayworth.) The music videos for *As I Am* exhibit far more complex cultural and political interests, along with textual elements suggesting how the objective of expanding her status as a black activist and celebrity is in play with her artistic production. In the video for the album's signature single (and Grammy winner) "Superwoman," Keys assumes five different personas, playing the roles of distinct black women. Beginning as a mother in a social worker's office, her two small children on her lap, subsequently Keys portrays a business executive (also apparently a single mother), an astronaut, an African woman collecting water in the desert, and what Keys's homepage calls a "Pharaoh"—an Egyptian queen on a throne. The video ends with a montage of the real women inspiring these personas. On the website, fans can vote for their favorite role depicted by Alicia. Musically, "Superwoman" shifts between the refrains "Yes I am," "Yes I can," and "Yes we can." The incorporation of individual and group empowerment calls on gendered subjects to draw on individual self-esteem and community pride. ("Yes we can" also echoes the signature phrase of Barack Obama's campaign.) By making these phrases a gendered call to mobilization, Keys conveys a very different message from the majority of her oeuvre, which focuses on the multifaceted role of love in individual women's lives. Songs such as "Superwoman" indicate that Keys is capable of expressing an explicit politics in her music, rather than relying on music videos to flesh out critiques about race and criminal justice, the challenge of retaining racial authenticity while pursuing class mobility, and so on.

Increasingly, Alicia Keys works to connect politics to her music career. In 2004 she co-founded an organization called "Keep a Child Alive," which provides low-cost anti-retroviral mediation to children in Africa with HIV/AIDS. In April 2007, Keys was the youngest person among a prestigious group depicted on the cover of *Vanity Fair*'s special issue on the African continent. Guest-edited by Bono, member of the internationally known rock group U2, "Africa" was an unprecedented magazine project. *Vanity Fair* published "Africa" with twenty-two different covers featuring twenty-three notable individuals, all prominent, powerful people who are active in improving conditions in the beleaguered continent. Interestingly, Keys managed to signal this political project in the video for "Teenage Love Affair," albeit in a way reflecting the troubled gender politics evident in the work.

"Teenage Love Affair" is an ambitious homage to Spike Lee's film *School Daze*, which depicts life on a historically black university campus (likely based on Lee's alma mater, Morehouse College). Curiously, the video omits a central element of the movie's plot—how skin color differences (more precisely, lightness and darkness) drive a wedge between African American women, one rendered more acute by normative heterosexuality. This decision raises provocative questions that elaborate on the conversation about how Keys and her team contend with her appearance. How do gender politics—specifically skin color among African Americans, affect the stakes of rendering Alicia Keys an authentic "black" artist? In Lee's original narrative, the student body is characterized by two intragender conflicts. The men are in oppositional ideological camps: political activists versus fraternity brothers. The women are divided by color, and the campus sorority does not accept dark-skinned women as members. The protagonists in "Teenage Love Affair," Alicia Keys and a character played by actor Derek Luke, find their relationship stymied because of Keys's reluctance to move more rapidly toward sexual intimacy. Two sequences in the video are faithful, virtually shot-by-shot re-enactments of scenes from *School Daze:* a clash between the two groups of men on the university commons, and a musical performance by light-skinned women members of the sorority. (Had "Teenage Love Affair" retained the theme of skin color politics, the analogue scene depicting the women's conflict would be a musical number called "Good and Bad Hair.")

Like "Superwoman," "Teenage Love Affair" is intent on communicating sisterhood, in this case across the unspoken divisions of skin color rather than "Superwoman's" clearly articulated hierarchies of social class. The question of how viewers unfamiliar with *School Daze* respond to "Teenage Love Affair" is difficult to gauge. As troubled as Keys's women in love may be, most of her music videos insist on their agency in relationships with men. In this regard, "Teenage Love Affair" is decidedly ambivalent. Keys literally hands over her "Keep a Child Alive" project to the activist men in the video; her protagonist admiringly watches Derek Luke representing the organization, exhorting the crowd to "Keep a Child Alive." The alluring recreation of the show-stopping women's number in *School Daze* is troubling whether or not one has seen Lee's film. The sincerity with which "Teenage Love Affair" steers clear of ranking women according to color (or, as *School Daze* depicted, hair texture) does not displace the video's unambiguous construction of Alicia Keys as the primary object of desire, albeit among other desirable black women. The classic signs of Hollywood glamour in this scene—Keys wears a fishtail dress, diamonds, and flowing hair—signals the beauty typified by black/white women and their "natural" ability to approximate white aesthetics.

As the millennium moves forward, media representations of Mariah Carey continue to serve the signifying function of the mulatto/a. In April 2005 she appeared on the cover of *Essence* magazine with the caption: "America's Most Misunderstood Black Woman: The story only we can tell." Carey appears as an ethereal blonde beauty with rosy cheeks and pale pink lips. The article begins by declaring that Carey bears no resemblance to Sarah Jane, the tragic mulatto figure of 1959's remake of *Imitation of Life*—the character formerly named Peola. This rhetorical move—litotes—works to associate Carey with the tragic mulatto even as it denies her resemblance to that figure.[47] The article delineates Carey's struggle to be accepted as racially authentic. Her friend Da Brat insists, "Hip-hop is in [Mariah's] bones, in her soul. That child is black. That girl is ghetto."[48] In a *Vibe* interview of 2003, Carey demonstrated characteristic insight into how her reputation as a musical lightweight—an artist known primarily for a pretty face and a beautiful voice—likewise begs the question of her authenticity. "If you're not strumming a guitar or playing the piano like Alicia Keys, people assume you're not involved."[49]

Interestingly, the question of Keys's command of Black English emerged upon the release of her first album. To the question of whether she slips in and out of dialect, a journalist confirmed: "while some question the sincerity of her ghetto vernacular, she insists it is all her."[50] The appearance of the term "ghetto" in media about Carey and Keys emphasizes the extent to which this term has been rehabilitated. Remaining aesthetically linked to the black urban underclass seems imperative for black men. For women, approximating the "real" is a more ambiguous enterprise. For Carey and Keys, maintaining their status as (hybrid) black celebrities demands the management of multiple markers of authenticity, including identity, musical idiom, and the relationship to black urban culture.

The inauguration of Barack Obama initiates a wealth of opportunities to theorize the vastly underresearched topic of mixed race and masculinity.[51] His candidacy and election spurred a tsunami of media that will occupy scholars for many years to come. The celebrity-studded Neighborhood Ball, which the Obamas attended, was one of the hottest tickets on the night of January 20th. Mariah Carey and Alicia Keys were among the elite group of artists selected to perform.

Keys and Carey have shared the stage for over a decade—especially at a number of "diva" gatherings, featuring popular women singers, televised during that period of time. Their presence at the Neighborhood Ball yielded deeper meaning. Carey and Keys are two of nine artists who performed both at Obama's inauguration and at the first benefit concert following 9/11. In fact they were the only women of color performers at the concert for 9/11. The notion of a symbolic trajectory beginning with the terrorist attacks on New York City, and ending with the election of Barack

Obama is inevitable and profound. A time of deep national mourning following an unprecedented attack on continental America contrasts with the election of the nation's first black President, a historical turning point celebrated throughout the world.

At the Neighborhood Ball Mariah Carey performed "Heroes," the same song she sang at the 9/11 concert. Her demeanor was strikingly similar and classically "diva;" she wore an elegant black gown and stood still before a microphone stand. Interestingly, Carey's personal life was again part of the spectacle. She and African American actor Nick Cannon, the Neighborhood Ball's DJ, had married earlier that year. Her whirlwind romance and marriage to Cannon, who is nearly ten years her junior, made headlines in April 2008. Celebrity media reported the marriage as evidence of Carey's unpredictable personality. Still, Carey's personal life did not eclipse the artistic resurrection of 2005's *The Emancipation of Mimi*, the so-called comeback album that gave new cachet to her iconic status and enabled her to secure musical relevance beyond the pop category.[52] *Emancipation of Mimi* edged Mariah Carey to the position of artist with the most number one hits—surpassing Elvis Presley and the Beatles. The hits "It's Like That" and "We Belong Together" received heavy play on black radio stations—both r&b and rap/hip-hop. *Emancipation* also won three Grammy Awards in the r&b category: Best Album, Best Female Performance, and Best Song (the latter two for "We Belong Together").

Alicia Keys performed the song "No One," for which she won Grammy Awards for r&b song and vocal in 2007. At the 9/11 concert Keys delivered a hauntingly beautiful rendition of Donny Hathaway's "Someday We'll Be Free." Accompanying herself on piano, Keys wore attire consistent with her aesthetic at that time: a lacy black scarf over cornrows. Her performance at the Neighborhood Ball incorporated important changes in her visual style and stage presence. Consistent with her more glamorous image, Keys's hair was straight and she wore a fashionable black dress. More important, Keys has made a practice of beginning her songs at the piano, but rising after a few bars to sing most if not all of her song onstage. Some music critics contend that her songs suffer from the shift to the stage. As an artist whose compositions establish intimacy with audiences, Keys seems to be experimenting with a more dynamic presence onstage, which does appear to increase her fans' enthusiasm. This transition speaks to the difference between delivering an artistically precise performance—what music critics listen for—and the multifaceted imperatives of celebrity.

As black/white icons, Mariah Carey and Alicia Keys seem to have started from opposite ends of the raced/gendered spectrum. Carey was perceived as white, then as a tragic mulatto, and in visual representations of the past decade is a textbook example of the virgin/whore dynamic. This particular oscillation between innocence and hyper-sexuality is gendered and related to mixed-race subjectivity. Carey, who has a room devoted to the Japanese animated character "Hello Kitty" in one of her homes, seems intent on creating the happy childhood she did not have, a past she readily attributes to the difficulties of growing up in an interracial family and as a child of divorce. (The film *Glitter* dramatized the odds against functional interracial relationships.)

Interestingly, media discourse about Mariah Carey repeatedly enacts a confrontation with the artist about representation and identity. Media as well as "gossip" about Carey seems determined to collapse the boundary between the sexually provocative imagery of her brand and Carey's own sexuality. Carey provided ample fodder for this accusation, including the revealing stripper aesthetic evident on her website, on the album cover of 2008's $E=MC^2$, and on a number of magazine covers and music videos promoting it. Carey insisted that the erotic and exhibitionist nature of such representations is a performance. She invoked "playing dress up" as the motivation for crafting these images.

Media discourse has also, for a longer period of time, implied that Carey's interest in black music and her connections with African American artists—especially in rap and hip-hop—are a form of racial passing, if not an example of expediency; a way of cashing in on her biracial identity. Carey comments on this discourse in her DVD "The Number Ones." Her self-confidence is an indication of the significant gap between the world of successful artists and the world of popular culture commentary. As Carey reels off the names of contemporary black musical icons with whom she collaborates, records, and performs—Sean "P. Diddy" Combs, the late Ole' Dirty Bastard of the Wu Tang Clan, Boys to Men, Jay Z, Missy Elliott—it is clear that the gossip about racial passing has little relevance to, and even less influence on, her creative work.

Alicia Keys has made moves from r&b/soul to pop and rock and roll. In 2007 she won a Grammy Award in the pop category for best collaboration with John Mayer for the song "Lesson Learned" (from *As I Am*). In 2008, she sang with Jack Black on his composition "Another Way to Die," the theme song for the twenty-second James Bond franchise film, *Quantum of Solace.* Keys experiences little if any challenge to her racial identity (although many who have heard her songs or seen her photograph likely have no idea she is biracial/African American). Keys's political activism is likely to increase her profile as a celebrity/role model, and bolster her already solid artistic credentials. The way she protects her private life minimizes her presence in celebrity journalism and tabloids. At this point, Alicia Keys seems to benefit from the default advantages of mixed race, without shouldering the burden of the tragic mulatto. For her, the movement into "adult" black femininity begs the question of whether she can maintain the edge evident in the videos for "Fallin'" and "A Woman's Worth," in terms of the politics of gender and social critique of racial inequality. Although "Superwoman" is an interesting and rousing anthem to sisterhood, both aurally and visually, the videos for "My Boo" and "Teenage Love Affair" are less auspicious. These more recent videos give the distinct impression that mobility for black women—at least as entertainers—necessitates a definitive transition to conventional feminine aesthetics.

CHAPTER 5

From Tragedy to Triumph: Dorothy Dandridge, Halle Berry, and the Search for a Black Screen Goddess

For me, it was clear that she was insecure . . . [a]nd obviously trying to achieve stardom in an industry that had no conscious place for her.

BROCK PETERS ON WORKING WITH DOROTHY DANDRIDGE
IN *PORGY AND BESS* (1959)

Wrenching tales of racism and sexism in Hollywood engender poignant examples of thwarted potential for film actors. Such is the case with Dorothy Dandridge, who at mid-century stood at an artistic tipping point in Hollywood. In 1955 Dandridge became the first woman of color nominated for an Academy Award, Best Actress. Her role in Otto Preminger's film *Carmen Jones* positioned her to become a genuine leading lady. The nomination gave Dandridge international acclaim, but could not compensate for the very few roles available for black women in dramatic leads. Even when Dandridge was cast, industry production codes and cultural mores prohibiting miscegenation limited her opportunities. *Island in the Sun* (1957) her second major feature, titillated the audience with interracial love, but downplayed Dandridge's erotic appeal. The film could not be screened in southern theaters without key scenes between Dandridge and her white film lover, played by Michael Rennie, being cut. Throughout her lifetime, Dandridge was forced to supplement her income with nightclub engagements. Ultimately, her role in *Carmen Jones* was the pinnacle of her film career. A combination of professional and personal disappointments, leading to depression and a reliance on prescription drugs, culminated in her death in 1965, at the age of 41.

Dorothy Dandridge's career was unprecedented because she seemed poised to enter the rigidly segregated realm of "film goddesses."[1] More than simply a role model, Dandridge is a citational figure—a cultural symbol that not only inspires widespread personal identification (especially among black actresses), but also facilitates the articulation of ongoing struggles over representation. This conversation was revived in 2001, when Halle Berry became the first woman of color to receive an Academy Award for Best Actress in the film *Monster's Ball* (2000). In her emotional acceptance speech, Berry claimed her award as a triumph for Dorothy Dandridge.

The positioning of Halle Berry as Dorothy Dandridge's artistic heir credits her with fulfilling the promise of Dandridge's career. This notion became naturalized in media discourse leading up to and following the Academy Awards ceremony, so much so that a linear trajectory between Dandridge and Berry is likely to persist as a feature of Hollywood film history. The celebration of these women as symbolic milestones and the incorporation of their careers into a narrative of racial progress laid the groundwork for an irresistible construct: Hollywood can make amends for Dandridge, its tragic victim, by anointing Berry as an exemplary and representative (African) American actress.[2] The figure of the black/white woman provides the traction for this narrative in the late twentieth century/early millennium. The 1990s' revised representation of the tragic mulatto converges with the extra-diegetic[3] context of the public's awareness of Halle Berry's biracial heritage to contextualize the idea that Berry is the logical heir to Dandridge. Halle Berry represents what her cinematic ancestor might have achieved under different historical circumstances.

The cinematic trajectory from Dandridge to Berry reveals how miscegenation went from unspeakable taboo to a lucrative site of commodification in the late twentieth century. The potent hybrid bodies of black/white women trigger the specter of miscegenation in ways that remain compatible with the values of a rehabilitated multicultural America. That both Dandridge and Berry are defined as African American reflects a continuity in how blackness is defined in American culture, as well as conventional casting in cinema. During her lifetime, Dandridge's blackness derived from the institutional enforcement of the one-drop rule. The criminalization of interracial sex and marriage, along with racial segregation, repressed the evidence of race mixture in the larger society by confining its effects to black communities.

As in many African American families, a legacy of race mixture was evident among Dandridge's immediate ancestors. Born in 1923, she had a light-skinned father and a grandmother (her father's mother) said to be indistinguishable from a white woman.[4] Dandridge's mulatto/a appearance even sparked Hollywood rumors of miscegenation; according to one, she was the daughter of the mysterious Madame Sul-Te-Wan, an ambiguous figure reputed by some to be D. W. Griffith's mistress and a white woman passing for "colored."[5] However, whereas tabloids delighted in gossip about celebrities in interracial relationships, race mixing and miscegenation were taboo topics in feature film.

Although Dandridge was a potent sex symbol for film audiences, to cast her opposite white men violated film production codes and the era's social conventions regarding interracial sexuality.[6] For this reason, the exceptional way in which *Carmen Jones* depicted racialized sexuality extended beyond the leading lady's magnetism; the African American press lauded the refreshing representation of the attraction between Dandridge and Belafonte: "movie makers are now casting a Negro couple a as love team that does not tax the imagination."[7] This comment points to the problem of conceptualizing sexuality as a normative practice when people of color are involved. The challenge encompasses racialized gender, intra-racial sex, and miscegenation.

In Dandridge's time, the threatening aura of black masculinity made it imperative that the sexual magnetism of stars such as Belafonte and Sidney Poitier remain muted. Under these circumstances, Hollywood could market Dorothy Dandridge as a sexual commodity far more effectively than a black male star or a darker-skinned woman—yet the industry's refusal to depict black sexuality prevented her from becoming a full-fledged love object for cinema audiences. The depiction of carnal passion between African American actors was limited, and most love relationships evacuated of any sensuality.[8] Interracial sexuality in film was similarly sterile and unconvincing, conditions the African American community discussed in popular culture.[9] These repressions in the movies posed a thorny paradox, for the very definition of dramatic leads is synonymous with sexual charisma.

By the 1990s and 2000s, depictions of interracial sexuality constitute titillating taboos that move products and attract audiences to films like *Monster's Ball*. Born in 1968, Halle Berry is the child of an interracial marriage between a white woman and a black man, and as such part of the "biracial baby boom" generation. *Loving vs. Virginia* had significant impact on Hollywood's representation of interracial relationships, a key aspect of both Dandridge's and Berry's acting careers. Halle Berry lives in a contemporary world in which the African American community has voluntarily adopted the one-drop rule as the standard of black racial identity. By the same token the 1990s multiracial movement's counter-narrative to the rule challenged that convention by self-consciously politicizing mixed-race identities, contending that biracial heritage should not be subsumed by archaic definitions of race.

Although Halle Berry's biracial heritage is well known among film audiences, she represents miscegenation—no longer illegal but still carrying a hint of the forbidden—no longer regulated by production code restrictions but still relatively rare and often controversial. In other words, miscegenation "works" for Berry, and actually facilitates her career—as much as it may also narrow her options. Moreover, the fact that she inspires the potent desire associated with interracial sex does not diminish her utility as a positive hybrid, an effective bridging figure between the races.

Halle Berry has a career that reflects the dramatic shifts in entertainment cultures that are evident in the post–Civil Rights era. As a young woman she successfully competed in beauty contests, winning the title of Miss Teen Ohio in 1985 and coming in as first runner-up for Miss USA in 1986. Early on, Berry achieved recognition as an icon of beauty for the general population, a status that Dorothy Dandridge could not compete for in her lifetime. Berry has the crucial advantage of ongoing work as an actress. More impressively, in 1999 Berry produced and starred in the HBO project *Introducing Dorothy Dandridge* (dir. Martha Coolidge). Berry won three prestigious awards in the Best Actress category: an Emmy, a Golden Globe, and the Screen Actors Guild.

Along with savvy career strategy and fortuitous timing, physical appearance is crucial to the apparent logic of Halle Berry's identification with Dorothy Dandridge. Berry established a concrete link between herself and the late actress. As a high-profile cable television project, *Introducing Dorothy Dandridge* made the actress newly familiar in mainstream visual culture, offering Halle Berry as an attractive proxy for the deceased star. Although the role garnered acting awards for Berry, the production relied heavily on imitation and verisimilitude to convey Dandridge's story, and the spectacular effect of Berry as Dandridge's virtual double is the film's key visual element.

In August 1999 *Ebony* magazine published the feature "Halle Berry: On How She Found Dorothy Dandridge's Spirit—And Finally Healed Her Own." Photographs in this article precisely reproduced archival photographs of the late star juxtaposed with Berry in identical clothing. As the article progresses, continual references to the uncanny resemblance between Berry and Dandridge enter the realm of the supernatural with the story of Berry being haunted by a dress belonging to Dandridge.[10] The virtual world of the Internet also touted Halle Berry as a reincarnation of Dorothy Dandridge. One website cites the actresses' shared birthplace of Cleveland, Ohio, and the proximity of Dandridge's death—1965—to the year that Berry was born—1968—as evidence of Berry's "soul mission" to ensure that Dandridge "finally (win) her award."[11] Such anecdotes correspond well with Berry's acting method in the production. The film's stylistic focus on visual citation and impersonation, along with extra-diegetic media discourse, illuminates the metaphor of haunting so crucial to the revision of the mulatto/a figure in the post–Civil Rights era. *Introducing Dorothy Dandridge* constituted an ideal referent for the anticipatory build-up to the 2002 Academy Awards, when a linear trajectory between Dandridge and Berry gained momentum as a cultural narrative.

Interestingly, the idea of a spiritual connection between the women had the effect of clarifying rather than mystifying Berry's claim to Dandridge's legacy. The impression that Berry was unique in her opportunity to "make history" was reinforced in numerous media articles. A number of journalists neglected to mention other black women who were nominated for Best Actress for films released in the years between *Carmen Jones* and *Monster's Ball*.[12] Although a number of young actresses in Berry's generation have sought to portray Dandridge, including Janet Jackson and the late Whitney Houston—formidable cultural icons in their own right—the emphasis on a virtually fateful symmetry between Dandridge and Berry effectively put those possibilities under erasure.[13]

Introducing Dorothy Dandridge faithfully recreated the conundrum of physical appearance for Dandridge, who, while celebrated for her mulatto/a beauty, found that few Hollywood films could accommodate her racially ambiguous looks. Film roles for black women tended to split along the color line, with dark-skinned women cast as mammy types and light-skinned women as tragic mulatto/as. Large, dark-skinned African American actresses such as Hattie McDaniel, Louise Beavers, Ethel Waters—and Dandridge's mother, Ruby Dandridge—achieved success in mammy roles in feature film, radio, and television from the 1930s to the late 1950s. On the other hand mulatto/a characters, while a staple in Hollywood film, presented problems in an American society with narrow views of black femininity and strong taboos against miscegenation.

African Americans were rarely cast as the "white Negro" characters in films such as *Showboat* (dir. George Sydney, 1951) and *Lost Boundaries* (dir. Alfred A. Werker, 1939). As Peola in *Imitation of Life* Fredi Washington was a notable exception. Film scholars rediscovered Washington in the 1980s, when Stahl's *Imitation of Life* resurfaced after spending decades overshadowed by Douglas Sirk's adaptation of 1955, starring Lana Turner. Fredi Washington's compelling depiction of a tragic mulatto/a became conflated with the woman, ultimately negating her potential to become a serious actress. Washington, unwilling to pass (a strategy that some urged her to pursue), or to accept the stereotypical parts that came her way, eventually faded from the Hollywood scene.

For Dorothy Dandridge and Halle Berry, viability as Hollywood stars derives from mulatto/a beauty—an appearance that is equated with refinement, sophistication—in a word, class. These qualities are crucial for a black leading lady to succeed as a simulacrum for the white screen goddess. Yet the screen goddess must also strike a fine balance between respectability and eroticism. For black women, this is much harder to achieve given the historical equation of black female sexuality with the lack of virtue. The privilege of light skin tone, then, is a double-edged sword. Dandridge showed herself to be painfully aware of this paradox. Regarding her nightclub career, she commented: "Ella Fitzgerald is one of the most talented people in the world. [...] And it embarrasses me that she cannot work the rooms that I work. The reason for it is so horrible. She's not sexy. The men in the audience don't want to take her home and go to bed. And she's up there singing her heart out for one third of the money they're paying me. And I resent being in that category."[14]

Clearly for Dandridge, the monetary reward she derived from being in demand on the nightclub circuit did not compensate for being the erotic object of white men. The successful commodification of black/white women in visual culture turns on the transformation of mulatto/a glamour into an appealingly lascivious sexuality. In effect, mulatta beauty facilitates the jettisoning of bourgeois class status and sexual propriety. Dorothy Dandridge detested that phenomenon on the nightclub circuit.[15]

Apparently, Dandridge's desire to become a serious actress outweighed the troubling prospect of being reduced to sexual object. *Introducing Dorothy Dandridge* recreates the tale of Dandridge's audition for Otto Preminger, which has become an essential aspect of her career mythography. As related in the miniseries, initially the director rejected her for being too genteel and ladylike. "You're very sophisticated. You're the epitome of high fashion. But this role of Carmen is one of an earthy girl that's entirely different than you are. Every time I see you, I see Saks Fifth Avenue."

Subsequently in *Introducing Dorothy Dandridge,* she convinces Preminger to change his mind by appearing at his office unannounced in a tight skirt and off-the-shoulder blouse—a costume more befitting the role of a sexual adventuress—prompting him to exclaim, "It is Carmen!" The film's historical timing was fortuitous. Released in 1954, the same year that *Brown vs. Board of Education* desegregated the nation's public schools, *Carmen Jones* heralded a new direction for African Americans in cinema. The story modernized Bizet's famous opera, transplanting his tale of Gypsies to a musical set in the World War II era. Dandridge's co-star Harry Belafonte called the movie the first all-Black film, "as opposed to a film in which Black characters played."[16] Although Carmen is a notoriously amoral and sexually aggressive character, Preminger composed scenes featuring Dandridge as the captivating focal point, constructing images underscoring her beauty and desirability.

Porgy and Bess (1958) was Dorothy Dandridge's second, ill-fated film with Otto Preminger. The movie depicted the marginal denizens of "Catfish Row," a southern ghetto. Like *Carmen Jones,* it was a musical featuring an all-black, all-star cast including Sidney Poitier, Pearl Bailey, and Sammy Davis Jr. The critical reception of *Porgy and Bess* revealed the contradictions that bedeviled Dandridge's ability to become a cinematic leading lady.

The light-skinned woman can be an enviable and socioeconomically mobile beauty, but her mixed blood is also equated with a compromised, wanton sexuality. The sign of mixed race connotes a fundamental tension between the presence and absence of female virtue. One could say Dorothy Dandridge collapsed under the weight of these incommensurable signifiers. She was classified as a mulatto/a star: too genteel to play a convincing black woman; too black to be white, and too white to be black. She was a leading lady limited to mulatto/a roles that exploited her sexuality yet prevented her from fully embodying the magnetic sexual allure of a screen goddess.

Porgy and Bess was a case in point, as numerous film reviewers complained Dandridge was utterly unconvincing as the prostitute of Catfish

Row. *Time* magazine wrote, "Dorothy Dandridge, who emphasizes the elegance of her bones more than the sins of the flesh ... makes something of a nice Nellie out of bad Bess." *Variety* chimed in: "Miss Dandridge is perhaps too refined in type to be quite convincing as the split skirt, heroin-shuffling tramp ... Dorothy Dandridge's Bess is rather too delicate, a sense of actual refinement somehow showing through the 'light woman' veneer."[17]

As black/white women, Halle Berry and Dorothy Dandridge embody a mulatto/a aesthetic, the neither "quite" white nor "too" black objects of desire. The sign of mixed race enables Dandridge and Berry to become icons of idealized black femininity. Halle Berry's success suggests that the dichotomies between white and black, between light and dark-skinned African Americans, that so limited possibilities for Fredi Washington and Dandridge, have shifted enough for Berry to craft an exemplary career. The late twentieth century's revision of the mulatto/a through the discourse of mixed race was decisive in why the narrative of tragedy to triumph, from Dandridge's troubling ambiguity to Berry's attractive hybridity, resonated at the turn of the millennium. With that said, complicated questions remain as to what the narrative arc of Dandridge to Berry renders murky or displaces, especially with regard to how Hollywood exploits the rehabilitation of the mulatto/a figure as a black/white woman. It is crucial to tease out the asymmetries of advantage and marginalization obscured by the accepted wisdom that black/white women embody an idealized black femininity consistently privileged in visual culture.

Halle Berry's strategy of subsuming her own persona in the service of Dandridge's memory made *Introducing Dorothy Dandridge* an effective bid for a place in Hollywood's pantheon of leading ladies. An essential problem remains, however, with regard to how the feature film industry constitutes African American stars. If the cultural norms and aesthetic conventions of cinema are structured to create white screen goddesses, the film apparatus cannot assimilate racialized figures as anything but simulacrum. Under these circumstances, black/white women clearly have an advantage because they more closely approximate the privileged standard of white beauty. By the same token, mixed race exists in an uneasy relationship with blackness.

As objects of the gaze, Dandridge and Berry are consummate examples of how Hollywood's standards of racialized beauty intersect with the intra-racial dynamics of appearance. Black communities make rhetorical distinctions between visual types through what I call a vernacular of color, where different shades of skin color are equated with gendered, sexual characteristics and socioeconomic mobility. Cinematic representations of Dandridge and Berry indicate some of the incommensurable tensions underlying how they have been incorporated into a narrative of racial progress in Hollywood film.[18]

Mulatto/a characters challenged the notion of degraded and amoral black sexuality, constituting, as Jane Gaines writes, "figures . . . representing the sexual virtue that black women were not supposed to have."[19] However, the claim that light skin color in black women facilitates access to the status of respectable womanhood is rife with contradiction As narratives such as Nella Larsen's novel *Passing* (1928) and Julie Dash's film *Daughters of the Dust* (1992) suggest, light skin color subjects black women to white male desire, and this sexual attractiveness, combined with their sexual vulnerability to white men, can negate their status as virtuous and respectable women.[20] This disjuncture is apparent as early as the slavery era, when light-skinned females were labeled "fancy women" and prized as sexual concubines. Harriet Jacobs's *Incidents in the Life of a Slave Girl* (1861) hints at the terrible fate awaiting slave women who are sexually appealing to white men.[21] Contemporary novels such as Gayl Jones's *Corregidora* (1976) and Valerie Martin's *Property* (2004) also thematize the destructive effects of white slave masters' obsessive desire for mulatto/a beauties. In many narratives of racial passing, the revelation of a light-skinned woman's racial identity changes the perception of her sexuality; white men no longer feel obliged to respect her womanhood, for blackness renders her sexual and available. Such a transformation is evident in work as early as Frances Harper's novel *Iola Leroy* (1895) and as recent as Julie Dash's film *Illusions* (1984), where the exposure of the drop of black blood immediately renders the mulatto/a vulnerable to white men's sexual aggression.[22] Even the apparently benign convention of "plaçage" in eighteenth- and nineteenth-century Louisiana, which formalized lifelong relationships between white men and their "octoroon" concubines, explicitly relied on the absence of sexual virtue among mixed-race women.[23]

Dorothy Dandridge constitutes an ideal referent for Halle Berry in terms of the quest to achieve the type of stardom heretofore inaccessible to actresses of color, and Berry's career-defining turn as "Leticia Musgrove" bears many of the troubling representations of black/white women's sexuality evident in Dandridge's film roles. *Monster's Ball* relates the story of a white prison guard who falls in love with an African American woman, the widow of an inmate recently executed at the prison. The film is set in a "new" South—a Georgia where the social veneer of civil race relations masks the dying remnants of Confederate pride and unrepentant racism.

Halle Berry has ascended the visual culture hierarchy, from television to target-marketed black cinema, to mainstream Hollywood, and is one of the few African American women to be cast in putatively "race-blind" roles.[24] Moreover, Berry demonstrates the ability to move fluidly between television and film genres. She has mentored well under her role model Oprah Winfrey, parlaying starring roles in high-profile television productions such as *The Wedding* (1998) and *Their Eyes Were Watching God* (2005) into multimedia opportunities that raise her profile among a targeted African American audience and a wider television viewership. In the new millennium, Halle Berry has risen to a rarefied realm that was, until recent decades, inhabited by few black icons.[25] Her Academy Award was instrumental in solidifying her star status and facilitating her steady development as a global brand.

James Baldwin's 1954 analysis of *Carmen Jones* eerily anticipates the visual impact of Berry in *Monster's Ball,* for in this film her "technicolored body" is most certainly "used for the maximum erotic effect."[26] Berry's buttery, caramel skin is a spectacle unto itself, amply revealed in clothing suited to the hot and humid southern climate: short skirts, short shorts, halter tops, backless blouses. As a woman living on the financial edge, Leticia is appropriately unadorned—she wears little jewelry apart from her wedding ring, her make-up is imperceptible and her hair simply styled. Yet Halle Berry glows, her "natural" beauty intensified by the phenomenon of juxtaposition. Berry is the luscious midpoint between white and black on the racial color spectrum in *Monster's Ball.* Virtually all the African American characters who appear on screen are played by actors with medium and dark-toned brown skin—molasses (Leticia's husband), mahogany (Hank's neighbor), blue black (Leticia's son). Likewise, the white leads are grayish and grizzled (Hank), an ivory that blushes easily (Hank's son), and the fragile, virtually transparent textured skin of old age and ill health (Hank's father).

Film criticism and media coverage of *Monster's Ball* routinely marveled at the decision to cast Berry as the unfortunate Leticia, tirelessly reporting the director Marc Forster's declaration that Berry had to be very persistent to convince him that she could depict a working-class, down-on-her-luck black woman. This commentary accelerated after the announcement of the Oscar nominations, when, for example, *Vanity Fair* magazine's "Hollywood" issue of April 2002 issue featured Berry under the heading, "The Surprise."

Notwithstanding the familiar stereotypes that cast aspersions on a beautiful woman's intelligence—the dizzy blonde, for instance, used to characterize Marilyn Monroe—does it make sense to contend that a "transcendent" beauty would impede acting ability? In fact, Hollywood requires "A-list" actresses to negotiate a complicated double standard with regard to the requisite beauty of a screen goddess and the acting ability of an exemplary artist. Does it behoove a woman to prove that she can act well without the "crutch" of beauty?

As more varied roles proliferated for women in cinema, numerous female stars have garnered acclaim for playing characters requiring them to minimize their good looks—"passing" in ways that deemphasized their beauty and feminine allure. Examples among Best Actress Oscar winners include: Hilary Swank becoming a man to play Brandon Teena in *Boys Don't Cry* (1999), and in 2004 playing plain-featured Maggie Fitzgerald in *Million Dollar Baby*. Gwyneth Paltrow became a man in *Shakespeare in Love* (1998). Perhaps most strikingly, Charlize Theron gained weight and wore dental prosthetics to pass as the downright unattractive serial killer Aileen Wuornos in *Monster* (2003). In an example of a role that also received significant attention, Nicole Kidman donned a prosthetic nose to play Virginia Woolf in *The Hours* (2002).

Would such a strategy work for Halle Berry? The possibility seems unlikely, for beauty and sexuality—whether high-class or wanton—are so enmeshed with the black/white figure as to be inextricable from what makes her a successful icon. The power of this discourse demonstrates how very narrow a platform exists for Berry to launch her bid for the status of screen goddess. As I have said, the black/white woman's ability to convincingly portray black characters requires a metaphorical "darkening" of the skin achieved by enacting downward class mobility, and a convincing transformation is enacted through sexuality.

This mechanism explains, I believe, why Berry's performance in the notorious sex scene in *Monster's Ball* was hailed as definitive confirmation of her acting talent. In the plot, chance circumstances lead Hank and Leticia to engage in a torrid sexual encounter that develops into a relationship. The graphically sexual scene was a crucial turning point in both visual and narrative terms, constituting the climax, as it were, of the film's exploitation of Berry's physical beauty, and a solid foundation of arousing miscegenous sex for the subsequent development of the film as interracial love story.

Monster's Ball ignited a controversy about the cinematic depiction of black female sexuality, with news media attributing to a number of African American actresses the claim that they had either rejected the part of Leticia, or would refuse to perform similarly graphic sex scenes. Berry's naked body had been on the public radar just the year before, when she appeared topless for the first time on film in the movie *Swordfish* (2001). That scene engendered a rumor she was paid an additional $500,000—or $250,000 per breast.

Whereas one can imagine other A-list actresses garnering similar attention for *Swordfish*-style exposure, Halle Berry's nudity in *Monster's Ball* triggers a specific historical memory of mulatto/a women as ideal erotic fantasy objects. That they are sexually appealing to white men constitutes the inverse of their status as proximate to white women and therefore possessing the virtue "that black women are not supposed to have"—for a mulatto/a beauty's sexual availability is proof positive she is not a virtuous woman—a lack which, along with the one-drop rule, racializes her as black. This circular discourse demonstrates not only the problem of racial color hierarchies that flatten complexities of gender and sexuality, but also the very limited space available for producing black leading ladies in Hollywood.

As an interracial love story *Monster's Ball* appealed to the preferred American narrative regarding race relations: personal relationships between individuals are the most effective way to transcend racial boundaries. In fact, the film convincingly portrays how deeply rooted racism remains under the smoothly integrated surfaces of institutions such as the prison where Hank works and the nursing home to which he commits his father. Hank and Leticia's emotional connection rings true. By the same token, their love is formed in the crucible of white patriarchal authority.

The secret at the heart of the film is that, unbeknownst to Leticia, Hank is the officer who guarded her husband the night before he was put to death, the so-called "Monster's Ball" preceding a death row inmate's execution.

Although Leticia discovers Hank's secret at the end of the film, she does not confront her lover. Hank, in the tradition of Strom Thurmond, "loves" Leticia yet does not ask her to marry him. He desires her, is willing to take care of her, even names his gas station after her—but in the end, Leticia achieves little more than the status of an octoroon concubine—protected and cherished, but deprived of the legitimate status of a wife. Ultimately, their relationship is a throwback to the dynamic between Thurmond and his family housekeeper Carrie Butler, a clandestine postbellum sexual affair that preserves historical asymmetries of race, gender, and power.

Halle Berry's recuperation of Dorothy Dandridge was read as the transformation of Dandridge's tragic legacy. Contemporary writing about Dandridge consistently conflates her status as an aesthetic mulatto/a type with heart-rending life circumstances. Beyond the example of her forestalled career, key details such as her mentally retarded daughter, numerous failed relationships with men (both black and white), status as a victim of spousal abuse, bankruptcy, and ambiguous death are consistently read as evidence of a tragic life. This narrative assists an actress like Halle Berry in the recuperation and rehabilitation of Dandridge. The powerful intelligibility of a trajectory from tragedy to triumph facilitates Berry's ability to restore Dandridge as a positive role model and, by winning the Academy Award, function as a proxy for Hollywood: the industry makes amends for its racist past by honoring Berry both as herself and as a reincarnation of Dorothy Dandridge.

Litotes—the deliberate understatement that affirms through negation—is ubiquitous in journalistic writing about mixed-race celebrities. Invoking the tragic mulatto/a figure is very often the preface to interviews with, and articles about, stars such as Berry, Carey, and Keys. Subsequently, the contemporary dilemma of biracials in multicultural America is layered over the historical antecedent. Berry presents an ideal persona for this cultural phenomenon. Although she has established an unprecedented career as a black woman in Hollywood, journalists frequently cite Berry's apparent fragility, the torment she experienced growing up in a household with an abusive (black) father (with whom she had no relationship), the identity challenges she faced as a young biracial woman and especially her unlucky love life, involving violent boyfriends and two failed marriages. While references to celebrities' personal drama are nothing new, representations of Berry inevitably focus on a type of triumph over adversity equated with her biracial heritage.

Hollywood's narrative of racial progress was particularly well served by the Academy Awards ceremony of 2002, where in addition to Halle Berry's triumph, Denzel Washington became the first African American to win the Best Actor award since Sidney Poitier forty years earlier, and Poitier himself received a Lifetime Achievement Award. The television cameras seemed to linger on Sidney Poitier with his white wife Joanna and their mixed-race children, and Halle Berry with her white mother Judith and African American then-husband Eric Benét. During Berry's protracted acceptance speech, the cameras returned repeatedly to her mother and husband, clutching hands as they tearfully witnessed her historic moment.

These images underscored the way in which nearly exclusively white worlds such as the Hollywood elite rely on a black presence to demonstrate their investment in the liberal values of multiculturalism and diversity. Interracial families constitute the ideal vector for such integration— a non-threatening variation on a normative social institution. Here the interracial family becomes the living example of a key nationalist ideology—racial harmony is not simply a futuristic fantasy, but actually exists in our midst. Moreover, prominent African Americans can be relied upon to integrate the nation, allowing all Americans to celebrate race mixing while adhering to the one-drop rule.

At the Academy Awards' Oscar night, 2003, master of ceremonies Steve Martin made a lewd reference to Halle Berry near the beginning of the broadcast—joking that she has had him served with a restraining order. Subsequently, while introducing Berry to bestow that year's Best Actor award, Martin paraphrased her statement of the previous year regarding how honored she felt to be the woman who "[broke] down this door tonight"—paving the way for other women of color to be similarly honored. Martin declared Berry responsible for breaking down the door "for really hot women in Hollywood." Berry then took the stage to announce Adrian Brody as the winner. What followed became a notorious, if not infamous, moment in Oscar telecast history. Upon receiving his statuette, Brody grabbed Berry, drawing her into a showy, swooning kiss that seemed to catch Berry off guard.[27]

Do sexual jokes and thinly veiled mauling come with the territory of being a black leading lady? Simply put, black/white women's sexuality conjoins white and black femininity in such a way as to guarantee perpetual desirability and availability. As the current pre-eminent representation of that fetishized body, Halle Berry reaps the benefits and suffers the consequences. Unlike Dorothy Dandridge, Berry benefits from the aura of miscegenation; it can be openly commodified in late twentieth-century and early millennial visual culture. Fortunately, popular culture's continual cycle of citation can respond and challenge the status quo. At the MTV Video Awards of 2003, Adrian Brody and Queen Latifah presented the award for "Best On-Screen Kiss." As they prepared to announce the winner, Latifah grabbed Brody for a passionate embrace—a clear reference to the "mauling" kiss between Berry and Brody. Latifah put a period on the kiss by slapping Brody on the backside, declaring, "This is for you, Halle."[28]

CHAPTER 6

High (Mulatto) Hopes:
The Rise and Fall of Philippa Schuyler

The signposts of birth and death delimiting Philippa Schuyler's short life seem predestined to make her an archetypal figure of the racial boundary. Born in 1931, the only child of African American journalist George Schuyler and his white wife Josephine Cogdell, Philippa began her life in the public eye. Her birth appeared in leading African American newspapers, including the *New York Amsterdam News* and the *Baltimore African American,* which ran the announcement on the first page. Schuyler's parents were part of the intellectual and artistic world of Harlem. Carl Van Vechten, noted patron of the Harlem Renaissance and photographer of its writers and artists, was Philippa's godfather. As a young child Philippa Schuyler became a famous prodigy of the classical piano, her mixed racial heritage playing a critical role in her public persona. Beloved in New York, outside the sophisticated urban center, she was a thrilling "colored" role model for African Americans throughout the nation. Philippa Schuyler died in 1967 in a helicopter crash while working as a journalist in Vietnam. Her death occurred just weeks before the Warren Court decision in *Loving vs. Virginia* banned all laws against interracial marriage.[1]

A number of high-profile interracial unions predated the Schuylers' 1928 marriage. Iconic figure Frederick Douglass married his second wife Helen Pitts in 1884, and controversial prizefighter Jack Johnson thrice married white women in 1911, 1912, and 1925. While not the first celebrity intermarriage to captivate the public, the Schuylers were unique because they were a fascinating family unit followed for years in the print media of the time. While modeling a normal, loving marriage and family, the Schuylers possessed entertaining eccentricities. Philippa called her parents by their first names; Josephine fed the family a raw food diet. (Today, they would be ideal candidates for a reality television show.) In the media, Philippa became the distillation of all that was alluring about the Schuylers—the charming and exotic, the appealing and odd.[2]

Today, George Schuyler's notorious political extremism competes with his legacy as a writer. Still his seminal works, the autobiography *Black and Conservative* (1966) and the novel *Black No More* (1931), are well known in academe. Among the scholars familiar with George Schuyler, most would be hard-pressed to identify his daughter. Yet for nearly three decades Philippa Schuyler's extraordinary intellect and her childhood as a prodigy of the classical piano made her famous among a significant number of white Americans, and a household name throughout black America. Following childhood stardom, Philippa traveled the world as a concert pianist, becoming a kind of cultural ambassador, particularly in the African diaspora. She also pursued a second profession as a published writer and international correspondent. It was in that capacity she died, in a helicopter accident while working as a journalist in Vietnam. Although Schuyler had by then reduced concert tours to focus on her writing career, and was two decades removed from childhood fame, her death generated the type of mourning expressed for major cultural icons. Among the multiple markers of Schuyler's passing that communicate her significance was a funeral mass in St. Patrick's Cathedral attended by more than two thousand people, with public schools in Harlem closed for the day so schoolchildren could witness her funeral cortege.[3] Years before, Schuyler expressed her painful experience of the color line as the paradox of a career spent performing for heads of state throughout the world, yet never being invited to do so for the leader of her own country. She longed to play for John F. Kennedy.[4] As if to assuage this unfulfilled desire, President and Mrs. Johnson sent flowers to her funeral.[5]

I analyze selections from the voluminous print media archive chronicling Schuyler's life and concert career to interrogate what she signified, in the decades leading up to the Civil Rights movement, to the two racialized public cultures, white and black, which then dominated society in the United States.[6] Throughout the decades of Schuyler's presence in media—from the 1930s to the mid-1960s—American media were basically segregated, with daily newspapers aimed at a de facto white reading public. Virtually every urban center in the country had at least one black newspaper (most appearing weekly rather than daily).[7] This vibrant black press performed a radically multifaceted role in African American public culture in the first half of the twentieth century,[8] voicing perspectives on overarching national concerns, supplementing mainstream journalism with ignored or suppressed information, and engaging the black diaspora. In addition, a significant number of popular magazines were published during this period.[9] Along with the well-known *Ebony* and *Jet* (a monthly and a weekly still appearing), the periodicals *Sepia, Our World, Hue, Flash,* and *Color* featured many black celebrities, including Philippa Schuyler as a topic and contributor. The declining significance of African American print media—especially news-oriented publications—is among the most dramatic changes in public culture since Schuyler's lifetime. As black journalists have commented, an irony of post–Civil Rights America is that while political change gave them unprecedented opportunity to report for white publications who turned to them as "experts," the higher salaries drew them away from black newspapers, a phenomenon precipitating the decline of these publications.[10]

The Schuyler archive is a capsule view of how media positioned mixed race under these circumstances—before interracial marriage and mixed-race identities became more a matter of personal choice than political statement. Schuyler is the point of departure for my analysis of how black/white women function as iconic and indexical figures in popular culture. Representations of her presage how media narratives about black/white women in the 1990s marketed mixed-race celebrity differently to black versus white audiences.

Schuyler's trajectory in media texts is marked by distinct stages delineated by age. Age is a crucial factor in the representation of mixed race. While the nation endows biracial children with a nonthreatening, mediating role between the races, this function acquires completely different overtones with the advent of maturity, when the black/white adult's developing sexuality makes miscegenation inevitable. Unlike contemporary images of black/white women, eroticized representations of miscegenation were rare during the decades of Schuyler's biracial celebrity. (A similar phenomenon would prove definitive in Dorothy Dandridge's inability to sustain a viable acting career.) For Schuyler there was no adult corollary for the niche she inhabited as a biracial child. Hence 1934–1948, when she was ages three to sixteen, were Schuyler's golden years during which she experienced her highest visibility in the United States.

In her transition from teenager to young adult, 1949 to 1952, Schuyler chafed under the child prodigy label, yet deployed the image to her advantage as long as possible. From 1953 to 1962, she built a career outside the United States, achieving world renown as an artist. While African Americans followed her global travels through newspapers and magazines, her white American audience shrank to metropolitan New York. I look closely at the period 1962 to 1966, when Schuyler assayed a new identity, "Felipa Monterro," with the goal of remaking herself as an "Iberian" performer. By this time, she was a published writer and correspondent. During these years she performed as Monterro, primarily in Europe. With a political outlook shaped by her conservative father, and increasingly out of step with mainstream African America, she also passed as Felipa Monterro in the United States—not as a pianist, but as a speaker on the far right lecture circuit. Finally, preceding her 1967 death in Vietnam, Schuyler's correspondence indicates a dawning recognition of the true nature of America's "Negro problem."

Philippa Schuyler's ongoing ambivalence about black heritage reveals a psychological assimilation of the prevailing attitude about race in America. Namely, the "race problem" derives from the *existence* of African Americans. Schuyler's own bitter words, written in 1963: "I am not a Negro, and won't stand for being called one in a book that will circulate in countries where that taint has not been applied to me . . ."[11] echo the frustration of Nella Larsen's biracial heroine Helga Crane:

> These were days when the mere sight of the serene tan and brown faces about her stung her like a personal insult. The care-free quality of their laughter roused in her the desire to scream at them . . . It was as if she were shut up, boxed up, with hundreds of her race, closed up with that something in the racial character which had always been, to her, inexplicable, alien. Why, she demanded in

fierce rebellion, should she be yoked to these despised black folk?[12]

Toward the end of Schuyler's life, she seems to have come closer to understanding W. E. B. Du Bois's brilliant take on the "problem." In effect, he reveals what the question should be: not "how does it feel to *be* a problem?" but "how does it feel to *have* a problem?"[13] In other words, the "Negro problem" is not the presence of African Americans, but white American racism. Schuyler's shock at the American military's treatment of black soldiers, coupled with distaste for their disdainful attitude toward the South Vietnamese army, attests to a late-blooming consciousness of race, as not simply a personal "cross" to bear, but a dynamic of power and politics.[14]

George Schuyler and Josephine Cogdell are an excellent example of the way historical conditions shaped social relations, making relationships between white women and black men a more likely prospect. Married in 1928, Cogdell and Schuyler met through *The Messenger*, where he was editor, and to which she contributed poetry and prose.[15] White women's greater autonomy, access to resources, and ability to live independently in the urban metropolis gave them opportunities to meet and develop relationships with black men of comparable educational background and shared interests.[16]

In the early twentieth century, miscegenation held a very different meaning for white versus black Americans, and had a different tenor in the North and South. Northern cultural mores did not entail a violent reaction to white-black relationships, making northern cities the most viable option for the Schuylers. Despite the reluctant clerk who processed their marriage license in New York, their marriage was legal. Although racial violence occurred throughout the country, the South's palpable hostility toward miscegenation was evident in the 1920s, when lynching increased for the first time since having steadily declined from its peak in the post-Reconstruction 1880s.[17] Still, interracial couples and families were subject to the same segregationist practices as African Americans in the urban North. The very existence of large black enclaves such as Harlem, where the Schuylers lived, confined African Americans to a limited space that whites could engage or ignore at will, making interracial couples and biracial children unlikely to disturb the normative racial mapping of the family. Whereas the cosmopolitan elite of northern cities might accept interracial unions, the rarity of the practice made these couples of little significant threat to the status quo. As a journalist writing for the black *New York Amsterdam News* commented in 1939: "The South, particularly the state in which Mrs. Schuyler was born, scorns intermarriage and denies racial equality; the North in which Mr. Schuyler is a famous writer, tolerates intermarriage and limitedly grants racial equality."[18]

For all intents and purposes, women like Josephine Cogdell simply "disappeared" into black communities, either rejected outright by their families of origin or, rather than facing that prospect, quietly ceasing contact with them. In her diary Cogdell wrote, "I have dropped completely out of sight . . . No one in the white world . . . knows my whereabouts or will ever know."[19] Stories of white families rejecting daughters like Josephine abound in mixed-race life narratives: memoirs by biracial people,[20] by white mothers,[21] and in family lore.[22]

Long a taboo whose results were confined to the black community, miscegenation represented a new frontier when interracial relationships were constituted within the respectable institution of marriage, and black news media featured the topic on a regularly basis. Respectability was a crucial concern, especially for the African American middle class.[23] Interracial marriage explicitly addresses the specter of illegitimacy that so bedeviled African Americans. The historical asymmetry of sexual relations between blacks and whites freights interracial sexuality with a complicated and lasting taint of shame, symbolizing black disempowerment under chattel slavery and the creation of fatherless, disinherited mulattos. As Hortense Spillers has argued, the black woman's body under chattel slavery was sexed without being gendered. Black women's vulnerability to rape and coerced sex with white men was reconfigured from a crime of violence to white men being helplessly coerced into sex by black women's excessive, primitive sexuality. Black men were similarly "un-gendered" through the emasculation of slavery; prevented from fulfilling the role of husband, father, and protector. The one-drop rule effaced white fathers of mulattos; such children became slaves.[24]

The transformative potential in interracial marriage lies in its ability to supplant the humiliating legacy of miscegenation through integration: through interracial sex as a practice that can be rendered respectable and the children of these unions legitimate through marriage. (Eva

Saks explains that the punishment for interracial marriage was often *more* severe than for interracial fornication. This discrepancy speaks volumes about state complicity in consolidating white supremacy explicitly through blood heritage.[25]) In the black press, stories about interracial marriages emphasized their symbolic value as signs of social progress. (Of the post–World War II period, Paul R. Spickard writes, "Black magazines paid attention not only to war brides and celebrity intermarriages, but also to celebrating intermarriages by less famous people."[26])

The Schuyler marriage was a critical refutation of archaic notions of race mixture. The Schuylers normalized interracial relations, enacting the final stage—marriage—that according to assimilation theory cements the integration of a group into the nation. As such, the Schuylers were in the vanguard of social change.[27] In 1939's above-referenced *New York Amsterdam News* article, "Interracial Marriage Is Workable—Here's Positive Proof," Thelma Berlack-Boozer, author of several features on the Schuylers,[28] emphasized their importance as positive role models for racial equality:

> She's a white woman. He's a Negro . . . Their daughter, now seven years old, is one of America's most gifted musicians . . . In this particular family you find exemplification of [. . .] a successful interracial union that disproves many accepted sociological theories about races and their interracial relationships . . . Happy ardent advocates of intermarriage, Mr. and Mrs. Schuyler believe it is one of the few things that will make this a more unified America.[29]

But even as many black Americans in these early decades of the twentieth century embraced white middle-class values and strove for assimilation into mainstream society, their general tolerance for interracial relationships was tinged with ambivalence. As Dorothy West's *The Wedding* explores in depth, although elite African Americans practiced strategic marriage in attempts to perpetuate physical features such as light skin color and wavy hair in successive generations, they disarticulated such desirable markers of race mixture from actual interracial sexual relations.[30] Social class was an important component of desirable white heritage; poor whites were held in contempt, a point of view contributing to the negative characteristics sometimes associated with whiteness.[31] Black objections to interracial relationships ranged from disapproval to opposition based on an inversion of the conventional racial hierarchy, where black viewed whites as frankly inferior and possessing tainted blood.[32] In the final analysis, whereas middle-class blacks were happy to claim elite white ancestry, they were not eager to "amalgamate." Black intellectuals maintained that, while miscegenation laws were an insult to African Americans, "amalgamation" was a white obsession. At the turn of the century W. E. B. Du Bois wrote:

> No, we are not demanding and do not want amalga-
> mation, but . . . it is not because we are unworthy of
> intermarriage. It is not because the mingling of races
> has not and will not bring mighty offspring . . . It is
> because no real men accept any alliance except on terms
> of absolute equal regard and because we are abundantly
> satisfied with our own race and blood. And at the same
> time we say and as free men must say that whenever two
> human beings of any nation or race desire each other in
> marriage, the denial of their legal right to marry is not
> simply wrong—it is lewd.[33]

Miscegenation laws were objectionable for their implicit signification of black racial inferiority and their distinctly un-American legislation of intimate behavior. As Eva Saks explains, miscegenation law constructed whiteness as an asset equivalent to property. The racial integrity of white-ness—blood purity—was essential to maintaining its value, along with all the privileges of race supremacy.[34] In 1967, the Warren Court pinpointed the primary objective of laws prohibiting interracial marriage:

> The central features of [the Racial Integrity Act of 1924],
> and current Virginia law, are the absolute prohibition of
> a "white person" marrying other than another "white
> person" [. . .] In upholding the constitutionality of these
> provisions [. . .] the state court concluded that the State's
> legitimate purposes were "to preserve the racial integ-
> rity of its citizens," and "the obliteration of racial pride,"
> obviously an endorsement of the doctrine of White
> Supremacy. [35]

Miscegenation laws' construction of blackness as essentially polluting makes them a key mechanism in the symbolic and material consignment of African Americans to perpetual second-class citizenship. As for the choice of a mate, that the state would seek to control something so personal is a critical point of reference in the Warren Court's decision. Their opinion concludes: "Marriage is one of the 'basic civil rights of man,' fundamental to our very existence and survival [. . .] Under our Constitution, the freedom to marry, or not marry, a person of another race resides with the individual and cannot be infringed by the State."

George Schuyler's status as a long-term correspondent for the *Pittsburgh Courier* and member of the intelligentsia made Philippa's birth a significant event—even front-page news—for black media.[36] Early on Josephine—by any measure a formidable stage mother—capitalized on her daughter's unusual precocity and her husband's respected status as a journalist by cultivating a close relationship with the New York press, annually inviting black and white journalists to Philippa's birthday parties beginning when her daughter was three, until the year she turned thirteen. These celebrations, orchestrated as media events to showcase the child's intelligence and musical talent were dutifully covered by reporters who returned every year.

The combination of George's high profile with Josephine's successful enlistment of the press facilitated how rapidly and thoroughly Philippa became a focal figure in the racialized news media of her childhood. In these early years, Schuyler was ideally positioned to function as a metaphorical bridge between the races. The biracial child is frequently viewed as an innocent being capable of defusing the tension generated by the miscegenous relationship. With her infectious charm and hybrid good looks, Philippa was precociously media-genic. A description of the three-year-old in 1934 highlights the feature journalists returned to repeatedly as metaphor for her magnetic quality: "She . . . walked in offering a polite 'How d'you do?' and a fascinating look from her enormous and liquid black eyes."[37] A reporter attending the final birthday party a decade later noted Philippa's "flashing black eyes, that became gay and serious by turn."[38] As a talented child whose mother was a tireless publicist, Schuyler quickly became ubiquitous in children's piano competitions, both "colored" and integrated. Her status as the youngest and most consistent first-prize winner in these contests raised her profile among black and white New Yorkers. Whereas Schuyler was Negro according to the one-drop rule, being the daughter of a famous interracial couple also made her biracial in the public eye. At this stage, her biracial heritage was framed by childhood innocence, a factor disarming racist sentiment repelled by interracial sexuality and defusing the disapproval directed at her parents' interracial marriage. (Contemporary memoirs by biracial authors note a similar phenomenon.[39]) Whereas she was, especially in the white press, depicted as an appealingly exotic little girl, one detects only vague overtones of anxiety about mixed race and sexuality.

Yet, even admiring stories about Philippa implied she was a fascinating biological and social experiment. Her birth in 1931 coincided with the growing influence of eugenics—an ideology intent on improving the human race through the isolation and eventual eradication of the "unfit." Eugenics went much further than conventional notions of inherent inferiority, targeting not only ethnic and racial populations, but also selected white Americans for sterilization: the physically and mentally disabled, the poor, the incarcerated. Whereas the obsession with creating an Aryan master race is most commonly associated with Adolf Hitler and the Third Reich, scholar Edwin Black makes a deeply unsettling, impeccably researched argument identifying the United States as the birthplace and most powerful proponent of eugenics.[40] The criminalization of interracial sexuality dovetails with the eugenic imperative to safeguard superior blood, and the perspective viewing "mixing" blood as a risky enterprise. In fact, according to eugenic beliefs, superior blood is always corrupted by inferior blood—with just one exception. Namely, in eugenics white blood enhances Negro blood.[41] In this way eugenics is compatible with the notion of "amalgamation," which demonizes race mixture, but also considers mulattos an improvement over Negroes because they possess white blood.[42]

In media representations of Philippa as the extraordinary product of a mixed marriage, she met the full criteria for what eugenicists call hybrid vigor—referring to "cross breeding" resulting in offspring superior to either parent race. The negative outcome of interbreeding, "hybrid degeneracy," refers to patently unviable life forms. In contemporary media, echoes of hybrid degeneracy are evident in depictions of black/white women as emotionally vulnerable, prone to psychological instability and being victimized in personal relationships, one example being Mariah

Carey's highly publicized "breakdown" of 2001. The discourse of hybrid vigor is reflected in ideas about black/white women's singular gorgeousness. Of course, both physical beauty and psychological vulnerability are also hallmark traits of the tragic mulatto.

Notions of hybrid vigor and degeneracy are evident in popular discourse about childhood genius during Philippa's lifetime, which featured a still familiar debate about the inherited and socialized aspects of intellect and talent. Child prodigies were a news-media staple, indicating intense interest in the debate about the role of nature, or inheritance, versus nurture, or socialization in child development. The concept of gifted children clearly had political dimensions for African Americans, who contended with the notion of black inferiority as an inescapable function of biological difference. The recurrent appearance of the "colored child genius" as a narrative in black media speaks to how important it was to counter these myths by disseminating images of exemplary children. These symbols of cultural pride became well known in black communities; and the media followed their progress into adulthood. The black community's fascination with Philippa reflected the impact of "colored" children mastering classical music—a white idiom—making them ideal role models, as mainstream newspapers regularly extolled the accomplishments of children excelling in classical music.[43] African American media looked to their progress into adulthood to disprove degenerate qualities related to genius, citing healthy lives and careers negating unflattering stereotypes. In 1952 Schuyler appeared on the cover of *Jet* magazine in an issue featuring "What Happens to Negro Child Geniuses."[44]

Media representations of the Schuyler marriage and Philippa contain overtones of race mixing as a fascinating biological and social experiment, conveying how discourses of hybridity influence narratives of political and social life. In the first prominent article about her, published in the *New York Herald Tribune* on August 3, 1934, the journalist references the idea of inheritance, writing that Philippa "comes by her talents naturally, for her father is a Negro writer and publicist, author of *Black No More*."[45] Articles pondered the source of her genius—was it nature or nurture? Josephine's unusual raw foods diet was a key aspect of the idea of biological experiment. As the *Tribune*'s Joseph Alsop wrote: the Schuylers "say that she is merely the product of careful education and a diet of raw foodstuffs."

Although the Schuylers repeatedly denied the notion that Philippa was a prodigy or genius, attributing her extraordinary talents to good nutrition and their method of child rearing,[46] Josephine was also deeply attached to the idea that her daughter was the product of hybrid vigor. The dualism of hybrid degeneracy and hybrid vigor came into play in an article published in 1939, the occasion being a concert Philippa gave in Philadelphia:

> Philippa Duke Schuyler, seven-year-old child wonder . . . had just completed the first part of her musical program, which consisted of 32 pieces [. . .] At eighteen months she was learning to spell at the same time she was being taught to pronounce words such as chair and Mediterranean [. . .] Meanwhile hundreds of little children, who had attended the recital with their parents were clamoring outside to get a glimpse of little Philippa [. . .] But her mother would not hear of it because it would excite the child too much, she feared [. . .] It was easily seen that with all of little Philippa's astounding stage poise and remarkable display of brilliant mastery of the piano [. . .] she was quite emotional and responsive. She did need care to prevent over-taxation of her little nervous system.[47]

Around this time, Josephine Schuyler's clippings include Charles Neville's "The Curse of Genius." Neville writes: "Thank your stars your Willie or Betty is just ordinarily bright, for Science, after twenty years' study, predicts a lonesome and often a tragic life for those so-envied smarties [. . .] The genius is often unsociable, and his romantic life is shadowed by failure to understand ordinary people [. . .] Average: He'll enjoy life, Average Plus: She will go far. Genius: His outlook is forbidding."[48] Josephine's marginalia reads, "This is nonsense." On the same page she has clipped and highlighted a short article from *Science News Letter* dated March 11, 1939: "Child Geniuses Grow Up to Hold Good Jobs."

Beyond being an intelligent and talented child, Schuyler was a real star, and like a star, she drew attention and generated delight in an audience.[49] Hybridity complemented her charisma; Philippa as adorable pint-sized spectacle "worked" in the 1930s.[50] As her biographer has written, Schuyler cemented a place in many people's hearts—so much so that she was presented to Mayor Fiorello La Guardia in 1938, and had a day named for her at the New York World's Fair of 1939–40.[51] As a double signifier—a figure of identification for African Americans and a pleasing representation of blackness for white spectators—Philippa inhabited the dual position occupied by exemplary hybrids. For the white press, mixed race made Philippa an enchanting oddity, a "less" different version of blackness.

Unlike black celebrities today, prominent African Americans during Schuyler's time stood little chance of ascending to the strata of "race-less" fame so evident in contemporary popular culture—at least, not without a significant cost. Black icons such as Bill Bojangles Robinson, Eddie Anderson, Steppin' Fetchit, and Hattie McDaniel achieved their fame by embodying the pernicious stereotypes of slavery days. Although singers and musicians were less constrained by racist imagery, their profession left them open to constant racial bias—performing in all-white clubs and, when on tour, subjected to the humiliations of black life outside major urban centers. Philippa was altogether different as an artist and entertainer. Although *Look* magazine dubbed her "the Shirley Temple of America's Negroes" the analogy's logic was based on her appearance—dark curly hair, radiant smile—and a similar quality of outgoing, captivating charm.[52]

Schuyler's performances could not have been more different from those of entertainers such as Temple. Her mastery of a "white" idiom, classical music, minimized the ways she might have been stereotyped had she excelled instead in a more "Negro" art form—say, singing or tap dancing. And, although the child Philippa was all smiles before and after every recital, she focused intensely while playing piano, one consistent sign of the oft-noted maturity of a serious artist. Descriptions of performances she gave at age seven make the point: "Because of the absence of . . . Anna Trockman . . . little Philippa Duke Schuyler of Harlem was called to the stage to perform instead. She didn't hesitate a moment but rushed to the front of the auditorium . . . She then climbed up on the piano bench, adjusted her position and calmly began . . . The applause, at the conclusion of her performance, burst out in appreciation. She was ready when called on!"[53] A different concert review remarks: "Her joy was infectious, her bows deep and perilous. She would climb, like the baby she is, upon the piano stool and then suddenly she would grow serious and grownup."[54]

In an extraordinary sign of Schuyler's significance, she was honored on a par with outstanding adults of her day. In 1939, she was among thirteen

"Women of Tomorrow" presented at the World's Fair by the Women's Service League of Brooklyn, "in recognition of their distinguished service to their race and sex."[55] Philippa's co-honorees included writer Jessie Fauset and actress/singer Ethel Waters.[56] The following year, 1940's "Honor Roll of Race Relations" acknowledged a dozen public figures, six black and six white, including Justice Hugo L. Black, Albert Einstein, William Grant Still, Countee Cullen and . . . Schuyler, again the only child in the group.[57] Schuyler, in her hybrid niche, crossed lines of race, age, and genre: she forged her own unique cultural space.

Racialized media make evident the stakes America's segregated publics had in the Schuylers. One striking feature in this regard is the language used to signify color. Mainstream headlines referring to Philippa consistently mark her with the term "Harlem:" she is "Harlem's Youngest Philosopher," a "Harlem Prodigy," a "Harlem Girl."[58] And, as her adult complaints attest, the other dominant referent for Philippa is her father, who in white media is invariably "George Schuyler, *Negro* novelist." Discursive representations of the family plot George and Josephine on extreme ends of the racial binary with Philippa positioned precisely between them. White journalists fixated on the physical contrast between George and Josephine. In *Time* magazine he is "coal black," and in a well-known *New Yorker* essay by Joseph Mitchell, "jet black."[59] In the same articles Josephine is "white," "Texas-born," and "a golden haired blonde." These descriptions clearly trigger images of the hyper-masculine black man and fair white maiden of the miscegenation nightmare—Josephine's youth as a southern heiress made the connection even more vivid. *Time* magazine calls Philippa "bright-eyed, coffee-colored." Mitchell's admiring words in the *New Yorker* paint a portrait of hybrid vigor: "She is a graceful child, slender, erect, and exquisitely boned. Her face is oval, and she has serious black eyes, black curls, and perfect white teeth. Her skin is light brown."

Notwithstanding the New York music world's love affair with "little Philippa Schuyler," New York's metropolitan papers evinced little discernible interest in the socially progressive aspects of interracial marriage. Although urban Northerners could congratulate themselves for being light-years ahead of the Jim Crow South, de facto segregation effectively created two stratified worlds without the explicit enforcement of laws mandating separation. Mainstream media tended to elide the social significance of the Schuylers' marriage and focus on their eclecticism:

cosmopolitanism, bohemian values, and the family's unusual raw food diet, a detail featured in virtually every story written about Philippa.

African American journalists also drew attention to the visual contrasts among the Schuylers, but only through comments about Josephine and Philippa. Not only would calling attention to George Schuyler's dark coloring be in extremely poor taste, there was no need to describe him; many readers were bound to be familiar with his appearance. The fascination with the interracial couple, then, is signified by descriptions focusing on Josephine's hair: her "blonde braids,"[60] that she is "blonde and attractive,"[61] or "blonde and exudes personality."[62] The black press also writes about Philippa's color, infusing the descriptions with affection: she is "golden brown,"[63] a "tiny brown prodigy."[64] Moreover, photographs of the family clearly communicate the visual spectacle of their color difference. Black and white news copy exaggerates Josephine's fairness, George's darkness, and Philippa's position between them on the color spectrum. The young girl's carefully coifed "Shirley Temple" curls also appeared as the midpoint between her mother's blonde chignon and her father's closely cropped hair. Although the black press identifies Schuyler with Harlem and her father, she is clearly a household name, and the implicit referent for a community persona. The headlines read: "Musical Genius,"[65] "(Little) Philippa Schuyler" and simply "Philippa."[66]

Like the white press, black newspapers entertained their readers with descriptions of the Schuylers' unorthodox lifestyle. The subtitle of Berlack-Boozer's 1939 article, "Harlem Family Radical in Views on Races and Food," promises entertainment as well as progressive politics: "Not only are the Schuylers emancipated in their ideas on race, but they're open and scientific in their views and attitudes on every avenue of life. They're as radical on food as they are on everything else. In fact, they are more scandalized by their pleasure in eating raw meat than they are by their intermarriage."

In black media, the Schuylers endured as a frankly theatrical family who made excellent copy. (Early on, Josephine's birthday parties for Philippa showcased her child's genius, but also presented her as a form of entertainment.) In 1951's "Meet the George Schuylers, America's Strangest Family," the magazine *Our World* featured an in-depth, tongue-in-cheek look at Philippa, Josephine, and George. Subtitled "with a raw fish and fruit diet, and their own educational system, they raised a genius," the article relates the Schuyler saga in a manner both affectionate and lampooning. Interestingly, the timing of the Schuyler marriage, along with George's famously contrarian personality, seems to have insulated him from what could be intense disapproval on the part of the black community toward African Americans in interracial marriages. *Our World* notes, Schuyler "was one of the few columnists to come to Walter White's aid when he was attacked last year for marrying a white woman."[67] White, long-time chair of the NAACP, was indeed vilified when he ended his twenty-year marriage with a woman of color and subsequently married Poppy Cannon. As a "voting Republican" George was by 1951 stubbornly swimming against the tide of progressive politics, which would become the Civil Rights movement. Unlike his daughter, Schuyler, though respected, was not a role model.

The article captures Philippa just prior to her second tour of the Caribbean, which would be her first time traveling alone. This would initiate a new phase in her life, in which she would explore alternative ways of identifying herself outside of America's definitions of race. *Our World's* take on her encapsulates the hybrid vigor/hybrid degeneracy dualism: "Fragile, pretty and as taut as a violin bow, Philippa Schuyler is somewhat of an experiment—a successful one." *Our World* cites Josephine's conviction that her daughter's talents do not only derive from raw foods, but are also a function of race mixture. The narrative implies that for all Philippa's gifts, genius exacts its own price—in her case, a life lived with two extreme parents. Her father's eccentricities are primarily political; her mother is a wild card. *Our World* concludes: "Of course, it might very well be that the only reason Philippa is a unique and strange child is because she has two of the strangest persons for parents."

As a child living in America's most cosmopolitan city, and as a driven artist sheltered from quotidian social interactions, Philippa reached her late teenage years without coming into contact with the garden-variety racial biases most African Americans learn to negotiate early on. Not until her first nationwide concert tour in 1948 did she experience overt racism, foreshadowing the ways America's color line would hamper her adult career. Shortly after that rude awakening, Schuyler embarked on a life-long international career which entailed traveling for months at a time. The years 1949–1953 marked her inexorable passage from child to young woman, and Philippa's exit from the idealized state of biracial childhood initiated important shifts in what the media emphasized about her. The question of age is crucial to how long Schuyler could retain cross-over status as a public figure whose appeal to white audiences lay in her precocity and unusual heritage. Childhood proximity between the races is, as Martin Luther King famously stated in his "I Have a Dream" address, a moving image of racial harmony. King's example works (at least for most Americans) because it is devoid of the sexual overtones driving anti-miscegenation sentiment and legislation.

As she made the transition from child to adult, Schuyler became imbued with adult femininity, especially in the African American press, where she was touted as "one of our most beautiful women."[68] Descriptions such as these make evident the way sexual maturity requires black/white women to become firmly anchored in a single racial category. Even as Schuyler tired of the "child prodigy" label, media from her first concert tours outside the United States indicated a deliberate strategy to slow the aging process. Caribbean journalists under-reported Schuyler's age by as many as three years. Long-time friend of the family Alton Adams wrote in anticipation of her St. Thomas, Virgin Islands debut of March 1950: "Philippa is the wonder child of the noted author-journalist George S. Schuyler," reporting her age as seventeen (she was six months from her nineteenth birthday).[69] The pattern would continue. In a review of Schuyler's Virgin Islands performance a photo caption of the "much-heralded teenage composer-pianist" identifies her as sixteen.[70] She ended her second Caribbean tour in 1952, the year she turned twenty-one, garnering a typical review praising "the incredible coloured pianist [. . .] Today [a] beautiful 17."[71] The Caribbean tours anticipate the painful conflict in her adult life between her rising position as a role model for the African diaspora and her deep ambivalence about black identity. Jamaican journalist Kitty Kingston wrote that Philippa was "regarded as the Negro hope to challenge the monopoly exercised by European piano virtuosos in the Concert field."[72] In 1952 the Cuban newspaper *Excelsior* published "1,000 Noticias en Sepia" (rough translation: 1,000 Notices, or News, for Black Folk), lauding Schuyler as a beacon for "la gente sepia" (black people). They called her "la graciosa americanita," and "la bella Felipa."[73] As always, the black American press avidly followed Schuyler's Caribbean tour, noting her impact on "la gente sepia":

> Down in Havana Pianist Phillipa [*sic*] Schuyler has
> really overwhelmed the concert audiences, plus. [. . .]
> The "plus" element of Miss Schuyler's visit to Havana
> refers to the lift she gave to the status of colored [the
> darker] Cubans, by what she did, how she did it, the
> social recognitions she received, and the honor paid her
> by the American ambassador and Mrs. William Beaulac.
> Harlem's own Phillipa, loved here and in the rest of the
> USA, increasingly the musical favorite of the Caribbean
> and, without forsaking her art, she is using her talents in
> a "plus" sense.[74]

Eventually Schuyler's image in the black press as Negro child genius
and potent symbol of a "workable" and "successful" interracial marriage
shifted to her status as the world's most gifted Negro pianist—a celebrity
in her own right.[75] During the 1950s and '60s, Schuyler maintained this
symbolic value—a figure of pride and admiration for African Americans.[76]
Yet as much as she desired success and recognition, she did not wish to
achieve it on behalf of "the Negro."

As Schuyler lost the ability to symbolize an idealized bridge between
the races, her appearances in the white press became more sporadic. Her
considerable success as a "child wonder" included competing in contests,
being singled out as the sole "Negro" child for broadcasts, and performing,
sometimes before integrated audiences and often under the auspices of
African American organizations such as sororities and the YWCA. Black
and white (urban New York) press coverage of these various endeavors
gave her a degree of name recognition virtually unknown, in the 1930s
and '40s, outside the realm of Hollywood film (hence, no doubt, the comparison to Shirley Temple). Opportunities became dramatically less frequent as she grew older. Schuyler retained a strong presence in New York
and other northern urban centers, where she played at prestigious venues
and saw her compositions performed by some of America's most famous
symphony orchestras. However, unlike black child performers, classically
trained adult African American musicians had no comparable alternative to the white classical music world, which excluded them. Schuyler's
childhood promise, especially as she consistently distinguished herself as
the best among an interracial field of young musicians and composers,

made her an ideal candidate to integrate the elite world of classical music. Instead, her artistic ambitions suffocated under the weight of American racism. Talalay's biography emphasizes Schuyler's bitterness at being frozen out of the conventional white recital circuit. Yet, although her absence from cultural memory is a function of historical exclusion, it is also a result of personal choices she made. Later in life, her attempts to subvert America's color line only increased her isolation and certainly contribute to her present-day obscurity.

Numerous scholars have analyzed the ways George Schuyler's extreme political conservatism eventually led to his near-total isolation as an African American intellectual. Philippa was strongly influenced by his political views, a factor which likewise put her out of step with her peers. I believe the way she was "forgotten" is also deeply influenced by her conflicted relationship to the black middle class. As a family, the Schuylers were in an ambiguous class position—upwardly mobile not by virtue of name or money, but through George's position in the black intelligentsia, the couple's progressive interracial marriage, and, as Philippa's fame grew, their daughter. Although her connection to George would remain an important feature in media, her status in the genteel idiom of classical music solidified the Schuylers' inclusion among the middle class. Through Philippa, news about the Schuylers would consistently appear in the society sections of African American media—where reportage on the arts appeared. Yet, despite access to the black middle class, Philippa Schuyler did not attempt to become solidly established among this group; her strongest association with African American institutions was limited to her childhood career.

How did other African American classical musicians—Schuyler's peers—cope with being stymied in the pursuit of a concert career in the United States? Archival sources about Schuyler reveal information about numerous artists and musicians, documenting African American classical musicians as private music teachers as well as professors in historically black colleges and universities. For example, a month before Nora Holt's story on Philippa's thirteenth birthday party in 1944, Holt's "Music Notes" column in the *Amsterdam News* reported on classical pianist Sylvia Olden-Lee.[77] Like Philippa, Olden-Lee was a gifted child musician and, judging from the photo accompanying the piece, very beautiful in a way resembling Schuyler, with light skin and long hair. Holt's article details Olden-Lee's accomplishments, including graduation from Oberlin

College, teaching at Dillard University in New Orleans, and touring with Paul Robeson. Olden-Lee married the conductor Everett Lee, with whom Schuyler would perform a decade later in Buenos Aires, Madrid, and Brussels.[78] Before her death in 2004, Sylvia Olden-Lee became the first African American to play with the New York Metropolitan Opera, and was renowned as a vocal coach. Other noteworthy instances of classical pianists breaking the color line include Natalie Hinderas, another erstwhile child genius who in 1953 became the first black pianist to sign a contract with a major broadcasting company, NBC.[79]

While Philippa Schuyler's decision to leave America was certainly grounded in a realistic assessment of the limited opportunities available here, these examples indicate that her frustration was a function of mindset as well as objective circumstances. Schuyler's deep unhappiness with being classified a "Negro" distanced her from the small community of her peers—other black American artists and intellectuals—resulting in a double foreclosure of opportunities within the black American community, along with exclusion from the white-dominated world of American classical music. Her racial alienation was such that she saw only the latter as a missed opportunity. That is to say, Schuyler chose not to capitalize on her access to the world of the black middle class—a world that included her, but which she seems to have inhabited primarily on the level of representation. Her presence in black media makes clear that America's "crown princess of the piano" would have been welcome among them (despite circumstances constituting obstacles for others, such as lack of a distinguished family name or inherited wealth).[80]

In 1953, the year she turned 22, Schuyler made her Town Hall debut in New York.[81] This recital marked her official transition into adulthood, and for the first time, the classical music critics who had delighted in her childhood precocity would judge her ability to join the ranks of professional performers. She could not put off adulthood as she had during her Caribbean tour as a talented teenager. Throughout her life Schuyler, far too well known to "pass" in New York City, likewise could not play fast and loose with her age vis-à-vis the classical music establishment. Josephine Schuyler's cultivation of the annual press pilgrimage to the Schuyler apartment for Philippa's birthday made it impossible to dissemble about her age. In adulthood, her white media presence, as always concentrated in urban New York, focused on her performances rather than her personality.

Schuyler's frequent and extended trips to countries in Africa during the 1950s and '60s and her work as a journalist for UPI and the right-leaning *Manchester Union Leader* (New Hampshire) gave her first-hand knowledge of the anti-colonial revolutions sweeping the continent. However, her adoption of George Schuyler's conservative viewpoints was evident in her views regarding Africa's inability to form democracies, and her anti-Communism. Moreover, due to her absence from the United States and lack of a fully independent life in New York she remained largely uninvolved in the profound changes being wrought by the Civil Rights movement. Quite to the contrary: from 1962 to 1966, years which saw Martin Luther King's March on Washington (1963) and Lyndon B. Johnson's signing the Voting Rights and Civil Rights Acts (1964 and 1965), Schuyler was intent on passing as "Felipa Monterro."

Ten years after being hailed "la bella Felipa . . . de la gente sepia" in Cuba, Philippa Schuyler (with Josephine's help) created an "Iberian" alter ego. She passed as Felipa Monterro, a classical pianist in Europe and England. In the United States, she lectured as Monterro on speaking tours sponsored by the American Opinion, lecture circuit for the ultra-conservative John Birch Society (of which George Schuyler was a member in good standing.) What was to be gained by passing? What Schuyler's biographer calls "the Monterro episode" demonstrates her attempt to capitalize on ambiguous looks and cosmopolitan life experience to craft an alternative ethnicity, one with enough "color" to account for her appearance, yet unconnected to African heritage. As an exercise in racial passing the Monterro episode reveals the nuanced differences between Schuyler, a black/white woman, and Monterro, a not-quite-white woman. Here racial passing points to the nuanced articulation of race, gender, and celebrity in the different sites of Schuyler's performances. The "racial" difference between the two female figures speaks volumes about the ways different countries—if not different continents—conceptualize blackness, Africa, and at that time, the American Negro.

In a 1962 letter to Josephine, Schuyler reported on her successful performances as Monterro: "If even music critics say I am obviously Iberian I must be! Not one person takes me for [a Negro!] and nobody in my whole life ever has unless it was written up in my publicity." Here Schuyler references comments made, for example, in the review of her 1953 debut on the European continent, in Zurich: "Le programme nous apprend que

FELIPA MONTERRO vient de l'Amerique du Nord: mais visiblement elle est d'origine ibero-americaine."[82] ("According to the concert program, Felipa Monterro is from North America; however, her appearance is unmistakably Iberian American" [My translation].)

Schuyler's triumphant interpretation of the reviewer's assessment of her appearance demonstrates her own fixation on appearing as anything but Negro. What she does not fully grasp is the reviewer's clarification that while she may live in North America, she looks Iberian—and hence not necessarily white, as in United States American, or white, as in Britain or Northern Europe. Northern Europeans at the time saw (and even now see) the Spanish and Portuguese as an essentially different, darker people. Elsewhere, Schuyler's statement indicating she would choose to be, if not American, French (or Portuguese) indicates her positive experiences as a woman of color in France in the 1950s and '60s.[83] Such comments indicate she was not exposed to virulent forms of European racism. James Baldwin observed that despite how well he as a black American was treated in Paris, "Algerians are the niggers of France."[84] The colloquial term for French people born in the Algerian colony—"pied noir" or "black foot"— indicates the ways colonialism complicated racial identity for the "authentic" French. The struggle for Algerian independence forced the French to come to terms with how being a colonial power engendered racial anxieties complicating their own national identities. Had Schuyler continued passing as Felipa Monterro, she might well have found the cachet of being black American was the key to her success in Northern Europe.

In the United States calling herself Iberian enabled her to capitalize on America's hazy definition of "Spanish." Schuyler's ability to pass as Iberian/Spanish resonates with fictional representation and real-life experiences of African American racial passing. Schuyler chose a racialized identity consistent with her hybridity, as well as leveraging her conservative politics in a receptive milieu. Monterro shared American Opinion lecture billing with speakers such as the African American reverend Uriah Fields, who "gave a background of the history of civil rights in the United States [saying] that methods of force, arbitration and integration in handling racial unrest have not been satisfactory."[85] The question of how Halle Berry's feature film will depict Monterro, virulently anti-Communist lecturer and apologist for European colonialism, will prove challenging. This little-known aspect of Schuyler's life undermines her suitability to serve as a role model.

The Monterro episode is key to one way Schuyler could be reinter-
preted for the twenty-first century: a sad example of racial passing on the
part of a tragic mulatto. The subtitle of Kathryn Talalay's 1995 biography:
"The Tragic Saga of Harlem's Biracial Prodigy," immediately triggers the
tragic mulatto, yet also makes expedient use of new identity formations
expressing reinvented notions of race mixture and the political rejection
of the stigmatized "mulatto" label.[86] Talalay's narrative historicizes contemporary race mixture through its revelation of an interracial couple and
their exceptional biracial daughter, important cultural figures of their time
and, as such, touchstones for contemporary Americans seeking to know
more about people of mixed race before the *Loving* milestone.

Afterword

For some readers it will be clear that the title of this book, *Tragic No More*, is a play on the title of George S. Schuyler's novel *Black No More*, which was published in 1931, the year Philippa Schuyler was born. On the surface, the relationship between this study and Schuyler's novel does not extend far beyond the title's wink and nod. That said, a number of intertextual themes link the two works.

To summarize the novel in broad strokes, *Black No More* is about the invention of a "horrible machine akin to an electric chair" which transforms black people by making them white (11). When it turns out that the former blacks are actually lighter in color than those who were born white, these "new Caucasians" are classified as a lower caste and characterized as mentally and morally inferior. To thwart this re-segregation, "those of the upper class began to look around for ways to get darker." Mrs. Sari Blandine, formerly Sissereta Blandish, develops an effective skin stain that she calls Blandine's Egyptienne Stain. "Everybody who was anybody had a stained skin. A white face became startlingly rare" (179).

The most salient connection between *Tragic No More* and *Black No More* concerns the way light-skinned mixed-race women function as avatars for Schuyler's scathing critique of the black intelligentsia. Schuyler posits sexual desire as the litmus test for genuine race consciousness. In the novel, Dr. Junius Crookman, inventor of the race-changing machine, "was what was known in Negro society as a Race Man. He was wedded to everything black except the black woman—his wife was a white girl with remote Negro ancestry, of the type that Negroes were wont to describe as being 'able to pass for white'" (35). Characterizations of numerous iconic figures similarly use sexual desire to signal political hypocrisy. In the novel, Dr. Shakespeare Agamemnon Beard (W. E. B. Du Bois) "bitterly denounced the Nordics for debauching Negro women while taking care to hire comely yellow stenographers with weak resistance" (65). Santop Licorice (Marcus Garvey) has a bookkeeper, Miss Violet Hall, who is "a pretty mulatto" (76).

In repeatedly lampooning the era's race leaders as hobbled by the Achilles heel of sexual desire for mixed-race women, George Schuyler shows how racial identity can be manipulated for social gain. There is no single tragic figure in *Black No More*. The generous sprinkling of "octoroons," "high yallah flappers," and "mulatto chorines" in the novel echoes cultural representations of the time and, crucially, types of black femininity. "Sweet Georgia browns" and "shebas" also inspire desire. By and large, Schuyler's women have no voices of their own. In this sense the novel, like the Race Men in it, is most interested in women as ancillary figures in a cultural narrative.

Perhaps no other discourse tells us more about the United States than the repetitive cycle of race. In recent weeks the media machine in Los Angeles, the city where I live, has revisited the notorious racial wound of civil unrest widely known as the L.A. Riots. On April 29, 1992, the city convulsed in a massive social meltdown when a jury in Simi Valley, California, acquitted the Los Angeles police officers charged with beating Rodney King. In April 2012, *Los Angeles* Magazine published a special issue, "Race in L.A.," with three different covers. Each depicts a close-up photograph of a young person emblazoned with variations on the same statement. One cover featuring a woman declares, "I am Asian. I am White. I am LA." A second, also a woman declaims, "I am Latina. I am Black. I am L.A." The third, a young man, states, "I am Black. I am White. I am L.A." One might say, to quote George Schuyler, that "America (is) definitely, enthusiastically mulatto-minded" (179).

Tragic No More has focused on mixed race, primarily in this twenty-year time capsule, to show how black/white women illuminate these multiple crossings between, above, and below the boundaries of race.

NOTES

Introduction

1. Karen Woods Weierman, *One Nation, One Blood: Interracial Marriage in American Fiction, Scandal, and Law, 1820–1870* (Amherst: University of Massachusetts Press, 2005); Alex Lubin, *Romance and Rights: The Politics of Interracial Intimacy, 1945–1954* (Jackson: University Press of Mississippi, 2005); Rachel F. Moran, *Interracial Intimacy: The Regulation of Race and Romance* (Chicago: University of Chicago Press, 2003); Renée C. Romano, *Race Mixing: Black-White Marriage in Postwar America* (Cambridge: Harvard University Press, 2003); Peggy Pascoe, *What Comes Naturally: Miscegenation Law and the Making of Race in America* (New York: Oxford University Press, 2009); Earl Lewis and Heidi Ardizzone, *Love on Trial: An American Scandal in Black and White* (New York: W. W. Norton, 2001).

2. Heather M. Dalmage, *Tripping on the Color Line: Black-White Multiracial Families in a Racially Divided World* (New Brunswick: Rutgers University Press, 2000); Kathleen Odell Korgen, *From Black to Biracial: Transforming Racial Identity among Americans* (Westport, CT: Praeger, 1999); Kerry Anne Rockmore with David Brunsma, *Beyond Black: Biracial Identity in America* (Lanham, MD: Rowman and Littlefield, 2008).

3. Kimberly McClain DaCosta, *Making Multiracials: State, Family, and the Market in the Redrawing of the Color Line* (Stanford: Stanford University Press, 2007); Herman L. DeBose and Loretta Winters, eds., *New Faces in a Changing America: Multiracial Identity in the 21st Century* (Thousand Oaks, CA: Sage, 2003); Heather M. Dalmage, ed., *The Politics of Multiracialism: Challenging Racial Thinking* (Albany: State University of New York Press, 2004); Kim M. Williams, *Mark One or More: Civil Rights in Multiracial America* (Ann Arbor: University of Michigan Press, 2006).

4. Baz Dreisinger, *Near Black: White-to-Black Passing in American Culture* (Amherst: University of Massachusetts Press, 2008); Michele Elam, "Passing in the Post-Race Era: Danzy Senna's *Caucasia,* Philip Roth's *The Human Stain,* and Colson White-head's *The Intuitionist,*" *African American Review* 41, no. 4 (December 22, 2007): 749–69; Leilani Nishime, "The Mulatto Cyborg: Imagining a Multiracial Future," *Cinema Journal* 44, no. 2 (Winter 2005): 34–39; Leilani Nishime, "Guilty Pleasures: Keanu Reeves, Superman, and Racial Outing," in Shilpa Davé et al., eds., *East Main Street: Asian American Popular Culture* (New York: New York University Press, 2005), Tavia Nyong'o, "Passing as Politics: Framing Black Political Performance," *Women and Performance* 29 (2005); Tavia Nyong'o, *The Amalgamation Waltz: Race, Performance, and the Ruses of Memory* (University of Minnesota Press, 2009); Naomi Pabst, "Blackness/Mixedness: Contestations over Crossing Signs," *Cultural Critique* 54 (Spring 2003): 178–212; Hiram Peréz, "How to Rehabilitate a Mulatto: The Iconography of Tiger Woods," in Davé et al., eds., *East Main Street;* Hiram Peréz, "Two or Three Spectacular Mulatas and the Queer Pleasures of Overidentification," *Camera Obscura* 23, no. 1 (2008): 113–43.

5. Sharon Begley, "Three Is Not Enough: Surprising New Lessons from the Controversial Science of Race," *Newsweek,* February 13, 1995, 67; *Time,* "The New Face of America: How Immigrants Are Shaping the World's First Multicultural Society," November 18, 1993.

6. "Post-Loving" refers to children born after the Supreme Court's 1967 ruling invalidating miscegenation laws in *Loving v. Virginia.* In *Racially Mixed People in America* (Newbury Park: Sage, 1992), Maria P. P. Root coined the term "biracial baby boom" to capture the rapid increase in birthrates for mixed-race children following the substantial increase in interracial marriage rates after *Loving.*

7. *Time,* "The New Face of America." A number of scholars have analyzed the *Time* cover. See Victor Burgin, *In/Different Spaces: Place and Memory in Visual Culture* (Berkeley: University of California Press, 1996); Suzanne Bost, *Mulattas and Mestizas: Representing Mixed Race in the Americas, 1850–2000* (Athens: University of Georgia Press, 2005); Michele Elam, *The Souls of Mixed Folk: Race, Politics, and Aesthetics in the New Millennium* (Stanford: Stanford University Press, 2011); Shawn Michelle Smith, *American Archives: Gender, Race, and Class in Visual Culture* (Princeton: Princeton University Press, 1999).

8. The draconian Johnson-Reed act of 1924 "based ceilings on the number of immigrants from any particular nation on the percentage of each nationality recorded in the 1890 census—a blatant effort to limit immigration from Southern and Eastern Europe, which mostly occurred after that date." "History Matters: The U.S. Survey Course on the Web," *American Social History Productions, Inc.,* August 25, 2011, http://historymatters.gmu.edu/d/5078.

9. Andrew Burstein, Nancy Isenberg, and Annette Gordon-Reed, "Three Perspectives on America's Jefferson Fixation," *The Nation,* November 30, 1998, 23–28; Orlando Patterson, "Jefferson the Contradiction," *New York Times,* November 2, 1998; Dinitia Smith and Nicholas Wade, "DNA Test Finds Evidence of Jefferson Child by Slave,"

New York Times, November 1, 1998, A1; Dinitia Smith, "The Enigma of Jefferson: Mind and Body in Conflict," *New York Times,* November 7, 1998, A15; Don Terry, "DNA Results Confirmed the Old News about Jefferson, Blacks Say," *New York Times,* November 10, 1998, A16.

10. Judith R. Berzon, *Neither White nor Black: The Mulatto Character in American Fiction* (New York: New York University Press, 1979); Hazel V. Carby, *Reconstructing Womanhood: The Emergence of the Afro American Woman Novelist* (New York: Oxford University Press, 1987); Barbara T. Christian, *Black Women Novelists: The Development of a Tradition: 1892–1976* (Westport: Greenwood Press; 1980); Vashti Crutcher Lewis, "The Mulatto as Major Character in Novels by Black Women, 1892–1937" (Ph.D. diss., University of Iowa, 1981); Elam, "Passing in the Post-Race Era," *African American Review;* Deborah E. McDowell, introduction to Nella Larsen's *Quicksand and Passing* (New Brunswick: Rutgers University Press, 1986), ix–xxxv; Earlene Stetson, "The Mulatto Motif in Black Fiction" (Ph.D. diss., University of New York at Buffalo, 1976); Jean Fagan Yellin, introduction to *Incidents in the Life of a Slave Girl by Harriet A. Jacobs* (Cambridge: Harvard University Press, 1987).

11. M. Giulia Fabi, introduction to *Clotel; or, The President's Daughter* by William Wells Brown (New York: Penguin Classics, 2003); P. Gabrielle Foreman, introduction to *Our Nig: or Sketches From the Life of a Free Black* by Harriet E. Wilson (New York: Penguin Classics: 2004).

12. Suzanne Bost, *Mulattas and Mestizas;* M. Giulia Fabi, *Passing and the Rise of the African American Novel* (Champaign: University of Illinois Press, 2001); Eva Allegra Raimon, *The "Tragic Mulatta" Revisited: Race and Nationalism in Nineteenth-Century Antislavery Fiction* (New Brunswick: Rutgers University Press, 2004); Teresa C. Zackodnik, *The Mulatta and the Politics of Race* (Jackson: University Press of Mississippi, 2004).

13. Cherene Sherrard-Johnson, *Portraits of the New Negro Woman: Visual and Literary Culture in the Harlem Renaissance* (New Brunswick: Rutgers University Press, 2007).

14. Lauren G. Berlant, "National Brand, National Body: Imitation of Life," in Berlant, *The Queen of America Goes to Washington City: Essays on Sex and Citizenship* (Durham: Duke University Press, 1997); Jane Gaines, "Fire and Desire: Race, Melodrama, and Oscar Micheaux," in *Black American Cinema,* ed. Manthia Diawara (New York: Routledge, 1993); Kathleen Anne McHugh, *American Domesticity: From How-To Manual to Hollywood Melodrama* (New York: Oxford University Press, 1999).

15. Marjorie Garber, *Vested Interests: Cross-dressing and Cultural Anxiety* (New York: Routledge, 1997).

16. Judith Butler, "Passing Queering: Nella Larsen's Psychoanalytic Challenge," in Butler, *Bodies That Matter: On the Discursive Limits of "Sex"* (New York: Routledge, 1993).

17. Julia Erhart, "Picturing the What If: Julie Dash's Speculative Fiction," *Camera Obscura* 38 (May 1996); Caroline A. Streeter, "Was Your Mama Mulatto? Notes Toward a Theory of Racialized Sexuality in Gayl Jones's *Corregidora* and Julie Dash's *Daughters of the Dust,*" *Callaloo* 27, no. 3 (2004): 768–87.

18. Adrienne Rich, "Compulsory Heterosexuality and Lesbian Existence," in Rich, *Blood, Bread and Poetry: Selected Prose 1979–1985* (New York: Norton, 1986).

19. Alice Walker, "If the Present Looks Like the Past, What Does the Future Look Like?" in Walker, *In Search of Our Mothers' Gardens* (New York: Harcourt Brace Jovanovich, 1983), 290–312.

20. Hazel V. Carby, *Reconstructing Womanhood;* Jennifer DeVere Brody, *Impossible Purities: Blackness, Femininity, and Victorian Culture* (Durham: Duke University Press, 1998).

21. Lauren G. Berlant, *The Queen of American Goes to Washington City;* Julia Erhart, "Picturing the What If: Julie Dash's Speculative Fiction"; Kathleen Anne McHugh, *American Domesticity;* Hortense Spillers, "Notes on an Alternative Model: Neither/ Nor," in Spillers, *Black, White, and in Color: Essays on American Literature and Culture* (Chicago: University of Chicago Press, 2003).

22. Toi Derricote, *The Black Notebooks: An Interior Journey* (New York: W. W. Norton, 1997); Marita Golden, *Don't Play in the Sun: One Woman's Journey through the Color Complex* (New York: Anchor Books, 2005); John Langston Gwaltney, *Drylongso: A Self-Portrait of Black America* (New York: Vintage Books, 1981); Adrian Piper, "Passing for White, Passing for Black," in Piper, *Out of Order, Out of Sight: Volume 1, Selected Writings in Meta-Art, 1968–1992* (Cambridge, MA: The MIT Press, 1996); Kathy Russell, Midge Wilson, and Ronald Hall, *The Color Complex: The Politics of Skin Color among African Americans* (New York: Harcourt Brace Jovanovich, 1992); Kathe Sandler, *A Question of Color* (Film Two Productions, San Francisco: California Newsreel, 1992); Judy Scales-Trent, *Notes of a White Black Woman: Race, Color, Community* (University Park: Pennsylvania State University Press, 1995).

23. Carl Degler, *Neither Black Nor White: Slavery and Race Relations in Brazil and the United States* (New York: Macmillan, 1971).

24. Hortense Spillers, "Mama's Baby, Papa's Maybe: An American Grammar Book," in Spillers, *Black, White, and In Color.* Numerous black feminist writers have theorized how the slave economy disarticulated black women's femininity from their reproductive capacity, rendering them female bodies devoid of female gender. See Angela Y. Davis, *Women, Race, and Class* (New York: Vintage, 1983); Paula J. Giddings, *When and Where I Enter: The Impact of Black Women on Race and Sex in America* (New York: Amistad, 1996); Deborah Gray White, *Ar'n't I a Woman? Female Slaves in the Plantation South* (New York: W. W. Norton, 1999).

25. Virginia's miscegenation law of April 1691 remained in force until the United States Supreme Court ruled the law unconstitutional in *Loving v. Virginia,* 388 U.S. 1 (1967). Cited in "Slavery and Indentured Servants," *Law Library of Congress.* August 25, 2011. http://memory.loc.gov/ammem/awhhtml/awlaw3.html.

26. Renée C. Romano cited in Kate Manning, "Crossing the Color Line," *Los Angeles Times,* March 30, 2003, review of Renée C. Romano, *Race Mixing.*

27. In 2010 the breakdown of interracial marriages was white/Hispanic, 43.3%, other mixed, 30.4%, white/Asian, 14.4% and white/black, 11.9%. See Wendy Wang, "The Rise of Intermarriage: Rates, Characteristics Vary by Race and Gender,"

Pew Research Center, February 16, 2012. www.pewsocialtrends.org/2012/02/16/the-rise-of-intermarriage/2/.

28. Roland G. Fryer Jr., "Guess Who's Been Coming to Dinner? Trends in Interracial Marriage over the 20th Century," *Journal of Economic Perspectives* 21, no. 2 (Spring 2007): 71–90. See also Kimberly McClain DaCosta, *Making Multiracials.*

29. Michele Wallace, *Black Macho and the Myth of the Superwoman* (New York: Dial Press, 1978).

30. Paul R. Spickard, *Mixed Blood: Intermarriage and Ethnic Identity in Twentieth-Century America* (Madison: University of Wisconsin Press, 1989).

31. Alex Lubin, *Romance and Rights.*

32. Hettie Jones, *How I Became Hettie Jones* (New York: Grove Press, 1996). Other interracial couples who met in bohemian New York include playwright Lorraine Hansberry (author of *A Raisin in the Sun*) and Robert Nemiroff, who married in 1953. See Lorraine Hansberry, adapted by Robert Nemiroff, *To Be Young, Gifted, and Black* (New York: Prentice-Hall, 1969).

33. Rebekah Walker, *Black, White, and Jewish: Autobiography of a Shifting Self* (New York: Riverhead Books, 2001).

1. Essie Mae Washington-Williams's Secrets and Strom Thurmond's Lies

1. As we enter the second decade of the twenty-first century, publication of memoirs by African Americans of biracial parentage (and mixed-race heritage) continues. Although the trend has slowed, clearly this aspect of the ongoing discourse about American national identity is far from over. A recent example is Bliss Broyard's *One Drop: My Father's Hidden Life—A Story of Race and Family Secrets* (New York: Little, Brown, 2007). Shortly before her father Anatole Broyard's death in 1990, the author learned he passed as white for most of his adult life. Broyard was a prominent writer and longtime literary editor for the *New York Times.* See also Henry Louis Gates, "The Passing of Anatole Broyard," in his collection of essays *Thirteen Ways of Looking at a Black Man* (New York: Random House, 1997).

2. F. James Davis, *Who Is Black?* (University Park: Pennsylvania State University Press, 2001).

3. Eva Saks, "Representing Miscegenation Law," *Interracialism: Black-White Intermarriage in American History, Literature, and Law,* ed. Werner Sollors (New York: Oxford University Press, 2000), 61–80.

4. The 1983 case of Susie Guillory Phipps of Louisiana (*Jane Doe v. State of Louisiana*) shows the persistent power of the one-drop rule. Phipps petitioned to change the racial classification on her deceased parents' birth certificates to "white" so that she and her brothers and sisters could be designated white. Some of her relatives, however, gave depositions saying they considered themselves "colored," and the lawyers for the state of Louisiana claimed to have proof "that Mrs. Phipps is three-thirty-seconds black." In 1983 the district court declared her parents, and thus Phipps and her siblings, to be legally black. In 1985 the state Court of Appeals twice

upheld the ruling (Davis, *Who Is Black?* 10–11). See also Michael Omi and Howard Winant, *Racial Formation in the United States* (New York: Routledge, 1994).

5. Lise Funderberg, *Black, White, Other: Biracial Americans Talk about Race and Identity* (New York: William Morrow, 1994).

6. Kathleen Odell Korgen, *From Black to Biracial: Transforming Racial Identity among African Americans* (Westport, CT: Praeger, 1999).

7. W. E. B. Du Bois, *The Souls of Black Folk.*

8. Marilyn Thompson, "Thurmond and the Girl from Edgeville: Old Stories have Reemerged about the Senator and His Longtime Ties with a Black Woman," (*Washington Post,* August 4, 1992.) In December 2003, Thompson got the exclusive to report Washington-Williams's identity prior to her press conference, again in the *Washington Post.* See Essie Mae Washington-Williams with William Stadium, *Dear Senator: A Memoir by the Daughter of Strom Thurmond* (New York: Regan Books, 2005), 217.

9. Ann Du Cille, "Where in the World Is William Wells Brown?: Thomas Jefferson, Sally Hemings, and the DNA of African-American Literary History," *American Literary History* 12, no. 3 (2000): 443–62.

10. Washington-Williams, *Dear Senator,* 211.

11. Shaila K. Dewan and Ariel Hart, "Thurmond's Biracial Daughter Seeks to Join Confederacy Group," *New York Times,* July 2, 2004. See also *Dear Senator,* 220.

12. The Public Broadcasting Service (PBS) has a comprehensive website based on their documentary, *Jefferson's Blood: Thomas Jefferson, his slave and mistress Sally Hemings, their descendants, and the mysterious power of race.* Included there is "The History of a Secret: A chronology of how the Jefferson-Hemings story was long dismissed by historians as legend, lie or worse." Just fifteen years ago the eminent historian Joseph J. Ellis wrote, "the likelihood of a liaison with Sally Hemings is remote." Ellis's comment appeared in *American Sphinx: The Character of Thomas Jefferson,* which won the 1996 National Book Award." pbs.org/wgbh/pages/frontline /shows/jefferson/cron/, accessed December 6, 2011. In subsequent editions Ellis has acknowledged the evidence and revised his position.

13. The Public Broadcasting Service (PBS).

14. Ibid.

15. Sharon Begley, "Three Is Not Enough: Surprising New Lessons from the Controversial Science of Race," *Newsweek,* February 13, 1995, 67.

16. David Mattingly, "Strom Thurmond's family confirms paternity claim," CNN Washington Bureau, December 16, 2003, cnn.usnews.com. Accessed June 15, 2008. In her memoir, Washington-Williams asserts that the Thurmonds' public statement referring to her "genetic heritage," underscored their impersonal stance toward her. See *Dear Senator,* 218.

17. Christy Oglesby, "Clash of Thurmond's public words, private world not rare, scholars say," CNN.com, December 23, 2003. Accessed June 15, 2008.

18. See Frank K. Wheaton, Esq. "Introductory Remarks: Essie Mae Washington Williams," December 17, 2003, cnn.usnews.com. Accessed June 15, 2008.

19. See transcript, *60 Minutes II* "Essie Mae on Strom Thurmond," interview with Dan Rather, December 17, 2003. cbsnews.com. Accessed June 15, 2008.

20. Dewan and Hart, "Thurmond's Biracial Daughter Seeks to Join Confederacy Group," See also Maurice A. Barboza and Gary B. Nash, "We Need to Learn More about Our Colorful Past," *New York Times*, July 31, 2004, and *Dear Senator*, 222–23.

2. The Wedding's *Black/White Women in Prime Time*

1. Oprah Winfrey uses the term "film" to describe *The Wedding* in her introductory remarks on both nights of the two-part broadcast. I use the term miniseries rather than film throughout this chapter to distinguish the work from a feature film. *The Wedding* was directed by Charles Burnett, well known for independent features such as *To Sleep with Anger* (1990) and Hollywood films such as *The Glass Shield* (1995).

2. According to Lawrence Otis Graham, Dorothy West's family was one of the first African American families to own a vacation home on Martha's Vineyard. The Oval is most likely a fictionalized representation of Oak Bluffs, the original and hence most exclusive part of "black" Martha's Vineyard. See Graham, *Our Kind of People: Inside America's Black Upper Class* (New York: HarperCollins, 1999), 154. Although Dorothy West's use of the term "colored" in her novel is historically specific, it is worth noting some African Americans (including West herself) have continued using words such as "colored" and "Negro" to define themselves despite the fact that such terminology is, in the post–Civil Rights era, seen by many as anachronistic, if not offensive.

3. I use terms that denote socioeconomic privilege, primarily "elite" and "middle-class," interchangeably throughout this chapter. "Middle-class," indicates an economic status that is associated with an ideological perspective. Although "middle-class" may be equated with "elite," the latter term more accurately conveys the broad range of factors that distinguishes privileged African Americans. Money is a necessary but not sufficient attribute for membership in elite African American circles. For the purposes of this chapter, then, "middle class" and "elite" are more precise terms than "upper class."

4. African Americans make distinctions among white Americans based on factors such as ethnicity, family heritage, and socioeconomic class, demonstrating Dorothy West's awareness that American whiteness is a dynamic classification to which people assimilate with varying degrees of success. As the plot of *The Wedding* makes clear, elite African Americans are strongly influenced by ideologies of white supremacy; they use prevailing white standards to define their own success. At the same time, they profess a contradictory "race pride" given their investment in a caste system among African Americans. *The Wedding* represents this essential conflict as a function of a tradition that younger African Americans are rebelling against, thus making them harbingers of the growing Civil Rights movement, a unifying phenomenon across boundaries of color and class to achieve equality.

5. Marlon Riggs's film *Color Adjustment* (1991) analyzes the reproduction and reification of racist stereotypes in African American situation comedies beginning with early television broadcasts. Spike Lee's film *Bamboozled* (2000) satirizes racism in the television industry and the ways racist representations of African Americans remain entertaining to American television audiences.

6. Deborah E. McDowell, "Conversations with Dorothy West," in *The Harlem Renaissance Re-examined*, ed. Victor A. Kramer (New York: AMS Press, 1987), 278.

7. In *Color Adjustment* cultural theorist Herman Gray argues that the mainstream success of *The Cosby Show* produced the enabling conditions for the production of sitcoms such as *Frank's Place*, which challenged culturally homogeneous representations of African Americans and explored complex themes of identity and difference. See Herman Gray, *Watching Race: Television and the Struggle for "Blackness"* (Minneapolis: University of Minnesota Press, 1995), 89–91.

8. The phenomenon of lighter skin reflects the strong link between appearance and socioeconomic mobility. See Graham, *Our Kind of People*, 7; Adrian Piper "Passing for White, Passing for Black," in *Out of Order, Out of Sight: Volume 1, Selected Writings in Meta-Art, 1968–1992* (Cambridge: MIT Press, 1996); and Joel Williamson, *New People: Miscegenation and Mulattoes in the United States* (Baton Rouge: Louisiana State University Press, 1995).

9. West, *The Wedding*, 71.

10. Ibid., 79–80.

11. As Shelby's sister Liz says of her baby daughter Laurie: "They brought her to me and put her in my arms, and I saw that she was brown. She was a completely colored child, without the protective coloring of the Coleses. I can't tell you how much I loved her at that moment. I wanted to fight the whole white race for her." Ibid., 93.

12. See Louis Massiah's film *W. E. B. Du Bois: A Biography in Four Voices* (1995).

13. Cultural theorist Stuart Hall challenges race essentialism by rearticulating a notion of black identity based on political resistance to hegemonic forces rather than on an imagined shared biological heritage. See "Minimal Selves," in *Stuart Hall: Critical Dialogues in Cultural Studies*, ed. David Morley and Kuan-Hsing Chen (New York: Routledge, 1996).

14. See William Julius Wilson, *The Declining Significance of Race: Blacks and Changing American Institutions* (Chicago: University of Chicago Press, 1980).

15. *The Two Nations of Black America* (PBS Frontline video recording, dir. June Cross, 1998).

16. *60 Minutes II*, March 17, 1999. CBS News Transcripts, LexisNexis, lexis-nexis.com/universe.

17. For example, Harvard professors Henry Louis Gates and Cornel West are depicted giving each other a classic "black power" handshake in *The Two Nations of Black America*.

18. The vernacular term "high yellow" is a designation that indicates light skin; it does not necessarily indicate that a person so described looks white. See John Langston

Gwaltney, *Drylongso: A Self Portrait of Black America* (New York: Vintage Books, 1981).

19. The photograph of Halle Berry flanked by Carl Lumley and Eric Thal appeared in *Jet*, March 1998.

20. See Alice Walker, "If the Present Looks Like the Past, What Does the Future Look Like?" *In Search of Our Mother's Gardens* (New York: Harcourt Brace Jovanovich, 1983).

21. West, *The Wedding*, 96.

22. Kate Manning, "Crossing the Color Line," *Los Angeles Times*, March 30, 2003.

23. Transcript, National Public Radio broadcast of Weekend Saturday (NPR 12:00am ET) February 21, 1998, transcript #98022107-214. "Interracial dating is still an uncomfortable issue for even the most open-minded black families."

24. Adrian Piper writes, "This is not to say that affluent blacks want to be white, but it certainly suggests that they have seen the benefits accorded to lighter-skinned blacks with 'whiter features'—who are hired more often, given better jobs, and perceived as less threatening." "Passing for White, Passing for Black," 377. And further, "Some people don't understand why a black person who was born with a good background of educated and well-to-do parents would want to pass, but I think it's more likely that we would try to pass rather than a poor black person because we actually get to see what the most privileged white person has in life. We have the same education, the same money, and the same potential. In a way, we get so close that it becomes an awful temptation." 383.

25. West, *The Wedding*, 49.

26. Fawn M. Brodie, *Thomas Jefferson: An Intimate History* (New York: W. W. Norton, 1998), 433.

27. Ibid., 239–40.

28. Ibid., 63.

29. Berry's television roles include the miniseries *Queen* (dir. John Erman, 1992), in which she played an enslaved woman who passes for white. In film, her roles include "authentic" black women such as the character Nina in Warren Beatty's *Bulworth* (1998), who provides a white politician's entrée into black hip-hop culture.

30. West, *The Wedding*, 212.

31. Brian Melley, "Races Mixing More in Central California than on Coast," Associated Press, May 3, 2001 (LexisNexis, lexis-nexis.com/universe).

32. See Lisa Jones, "Looking for Mariah," in *Bulletproof Diva: Tales of Race, Sex, and Hair* (New York: Doubleday, 1994). Tiger Woods was excoriated for his proclaimed "Cablinasian" identity (a term that he created to indicate his mixed Caucasian, black and Asian ancestry). See Terence Moore, "Wake Up Tiger, This Is American and That Means You're Black," *Atlanta Journal Constitution*, April 25, 1997.

33. See G. Reginald Daniel, "Passers and Pluralists: Subverting the Racial Divide," in *Racially Mixed People in America*, 91–107.

34. Adrian Piper identifies both in literature and in everyday life an assumption that

there is "a mysterious and inchoate essence of blackness that only other blacks have the antennae to detect." See Piper, "Passing for White, Passing for Black," 278.

35. The *Oprah Winfrey Show,* February 20, 1998.

36. Henry Louis Gates Jr., "Beyond the Color Line," *New Yorker,* September 17, 1998, 82.

3. Sex and Femininity in Danzy Senna's Novels

1. Sara Evans, *Personal Politics: The Roots of Women's Liberation in the Civil Rights Movement and the New Left* (New York: Knopf, 1979) on how white women's personal and political lives were transformed by their participation in movements for racial justice.

2. The white community's rejection of white women in interracial relationships appears in the earliest African American literature; one example is Harriet Wilson's depiction of Mag Smith, the white washerwoman who is the mother of the mulatto/a protagonist. See P. Gabrielle Foreman's "Introduction" in *Our Nig: or, Sketches from the Life of a Free Black,* ed. Foreman and Reginald H. Pitts (New York: Penguin Classics, 2008).

3. That the color line will disappear as a function of interracial sexuality and the mixed-race body is a persistent notion, expressed as the conviction that once everyone becomes "the same color" racism will come to an end. Ngozi Onwurah's 1991 film *Coffee Coloured Children* makes astute commentary on this discourse in the context of British society (New York: Women Make Movies).

4. Werner Sollors uses the term "calculus of color" to describe the ways that the United States quantifies so-called black blood, a definition that does not challenge the implicit assumption that, for example, quadroons are lighter than mulattoes but darker than octoroons. *Neither Black Nor White Yet Both* (New York: Oxford University Press, 1997). By contrast, African American color terms tend to be based on appearance rather than blood heritage. A particularly humorous example of an African American calculus of color appears in Fran Ross's novel *Oreo.* The author concocts a numbered color scale corresponding with colloquialisms such as "high yellow (pronounced YAL-la" (a 2), "light-skinned" (a 4) and "dark brown-skinned (a 7). Fran Ross, *Oreo* (Boston: Northeastern University Press, 2000), 5.

5. Helga Crane's appearance does not seem African to everyone. In *Quicksand,* a Danish woman in Copenhagen refuses to believe Helga is a Negro "for she knew as well as everyone else that Negroes were black and had wooly hair." Nella Larsen, *Quicksand and Passing,* ed. Deborah E. McDowell (New Brunswick: Rutgers University Press, 1986), 78.

6. In *Africans and Native Americans: The Language of Race and the Evolution of Red-Black Peoples* (Champaign: University of Illinois Press, 1993), Jack D. Forbes mobilizes extensive historical research to show the term "mulatto" was used in the eighteenth and nineteenth century to refer to people of African and Native American descent in the United States.

7. Danzy Senna, *Caucasia* (New York, Riverhead Books, 1998), 34.

8. Angela Y. Davis, "Afro Images: Politics, Fashion, and Nostalgia," *The Angela Y. Davis Reader,* ed. Joy James (Malden, MA: Blackwell, 1998), 273.

9. Senna, *Caucasia,* 196.

10. Michele Elam, "Passing in the Post-Race Era." *African American Review* 41, no. 4 (Winter 2007): 749–69.

11. Senna, *Caucasia,* 29.

12. Ibid., 56.

13. Ibid., 135.

14. F. James Davis remarks, "For many years the federal courts kept ruling that people from India are not Caucasian, but finally held that they are." F. James Davis, *Who Is Black? One Nation's Definition* (University Park: Pennsylvania State University Press, 2001), 159.

15. Mark Broyard and Roger Guenevere Smith's stage play *Inside the Creole Mafia* incisively lampoons the Creole preference for French rather than Spanish heritage.

16. John Langston Gwaltney, *Drylongso: A Self-Portrait of Black America.*

17. Thanks to Tara Lake for this insight.

18. Senna, *Caucasia,* 45.

19. Ibid., 48.

20. Ibid., 63.

21. Ibid., 66.

22. William Wells Brown, *Clotel; or, The President's Daughter,* ed. M. Giula Fabi (Penguin Classics, 2003).

23. *Imitation of Life,* directed by John Stahl, was adapted from the 1933 novel by Fannie Hurst.

24. Larsen, *Quicksand and Passing,* 39–40.

25. Senna, *Caucasia,* 248.

26. Jennifer DeVere Brody, "Memory's Movements: Minstrelsy, Miscegenation, and American Race Studies," *American Literary History* 11, no. 4 (Winter 1999): 736–45.

27. Senna, *Caucasia,* 204–5.

28. Ibid., 223.

29. Ibid., 235–37.

30. Ibid., 48.

31. Davis, *Who Is Black?;* Adrian Piper, "Passing for Black, Passing for White."

32. Virtually white-appearing performance artist Adrian Piper performs "My Calling Card," which involves letting people know she is black when they make racist comments. Piper, *Out of Order, Out of Sight.*

33. Senna, *Caucasia,* 274.

34. Birdie's glimpse of hip-hop music re-ignites her own desire for black culture and reveals Mona and Jim's fear of the urban black world.

35. Danzy Senna, *Symptomatic* (New York: Penguin, 2004), 184.

36. Ibid., 224.

37. Everett P. Stonequist, *The Marginal Man: A Study in Personality and Culture Conflict* (New York: Charles Scribner's Sons, 1937).

38. Senna, *Symptomatic*, 46.

39. Ibid., 48.

40. Senna, *Caucasia*, 412.

41. Senna, *Symptomatic*, 202.

42. Ibid., 35.

43. Ibid., 143.

44. Piper, "Passing for White, Passing for Black," 276.

45. Senna, *Symptomatic*, 103.

46. Maria P. P. Root, "A Bill of Rights for Racially Mixed People," *The Multiracial Experience: Racial Borders as the New Frontier* (Thousand Oaks, CA: Sage, 1996), 7.

47. Piper, "Passing for White, Passing for Black," 280.

48. Peggy MacIntosh, "White Privilege: Unpacking the Invisible Knapsack," *Peace and Freedom,* July/August 1989.

49. Robert Bonazzi, *Man in the Mirror: John Howard Griffin and the Story of Black Like Me* (Maryknoll, NY: Orbis Books, 1997), 42.

50. Ibid., 38.

51. Senna, *Symptomatic*, 413.

4. Faking the Funk? Mariah Carey, Alicia Keys, and the Politics of Passing

1. Hazel V. Carby, *Reconstructing Womanhood,* 89.

2. Homi K. Bhabha, "Foreword: Remembering Fanon: Self, Psyche, and the Colonial Condition," in Frantz Fanon, *Black Skin, White Masks* (London: Pluto, 1986).

3. Cynthia Nakashima, "An Invisible Monster: The Creation and Denial of Mixed-Race People in America," and Carla K. Bradshaw, "Beauty and the Beast: On Racial Ambiguity," both in *Racially Mixed People in America,* ed. Maria P. P. Root.

4. The fetish for light-skinned women—"quadroons" and "octoroons"—and the notion they made ideal concubines was institutionalized in the nineteenth-century New Orleans practice of plaçage, in which wealthy (white) Creole men chose partners from among the mixed-race women of the free black community. See Monique Guillory, "Under One Roof: The Sins and Sanctities of the New Orleans Quadroon Balls," in *Race Consciousness: African American Studies for the New Century,* ed. Judith Jackson Fossett and Jeffrey A. Tucker (New York: New York University Press, 1997).

5. Mariah Carey was the best-selling female recording artist of the 1990s, with more number one singles than any other woman artist in history and surpassed in number one hits on the charts only by the Beatles and Elvis Presley. Carey negotiated an early release from her contract with Columbia and brokered her own record deal with Virgin Records in 2001. Her new agreement paid her 23 million dollars for the *Glitter* album soundtrack before record executives heard a single note. In the weeks following the United States entry into the war with Afghanistan, Carey appeared to be recovering from the humiliation of her film flop, ignoring her scapegoat status

by traveling to Bosnia and entertaining American troops, being photographed on the shoulders of American soldiers resplendent in cleavage-baring khaki fatigues. Subsequently, however, her record company paid Carey 28 million dollars to release the label from her contract following the disappointing sales of the *Glitter* album.

6. The press reported that *Glitter* was no greater a financial debacle than contemporaneous films starring musical artists, including a project with members of the boy band N'Sync and two films featuring Snoop Dogg, *Bones* and *The Wash* (both 2001). The vitriol reserved for the commercial failure of Mariah Carey's film would seem to reflect not only the ambivalence directed toward her as a hybrid figure but also the considerable misogyny which at that time seemed linked to her status as a "pop" rather than "soul" or "hip-hop" diva. See Nick Madigan, "Pop Stars Try to Parlay Fame into Big-Screen Success, but Few Quit Their Day Job," *New York Times*, March 6, 2002, B1.

7. Noel Holston, "Viewers Get a Dose of Comic Relief; Late-night Shows Struggle to Find Humor after the Tragedy," *Newsday*, October 1, 2001, Part II, p. B02.

8. IMDb, The Internet Movie Database.

9. Victor Burgin, *In/Different Spaces: Place and Memory in Visual Culture* (Berkeley: University of California Press, 1996), 257.

10. Lisa Jones, *Bulletproof Diva: Tales of Race, Sex, and Hair* (New York: Doubleday, 1994).

11. Connie Johnson, "Pop Beat/Soul: Kipper Jones' 'Ordinary Story' Is Anything But," *Los Angeles Times*, July 28, 1990, F (20) 5.

12. Dennis Hunt, "Pop Music; Mixed Media: Mariah Carey: The First Vision," *Los Angeles Times*, March 17, 1991, Calendar, 64.

13. Lynn Norent, "Mariah Carey: 'Not Another White Girl Trying to Sing Black,'" *Ebony*, March 1991, 54.

14. Carey's appearances on the talk shows were excerpted in the VH1 documentary *Mariah Carey's Greatest TV Moments*.

15. Adrian Piper, "Passing for White, Passing for Black," 292.

16. For example, the film *True Lies* (dir. James Cameron, 1994) contains an arresting scene in which one character taunts another that Sicilians are "niggers." Scholars have written about the identification that much "gangsta" rap music expresses with Italian American iconography through citing images that derive from mobster vernacular. John Gennari, "Passing for Italian," *Transition* 72, 6, no. 4 (Winter 1996): 36–49.

17. "Who am I? Mixed Race and Passing," *The Ananda Lewis Show*, exec. Prod. David Armour, KTVU-TV Fox (San Francisco), broadcast October 29, 2001. Provocatively, the show's synopsis defined "passing" as "being biracial, and passing as only one race." The original source for this information was theanandalewisshow. com. The website is no longer online as the show was canceled in 2002. The source for information about the show's cancellation is the website www.tvtome.com.

18. Jones, *Bulletproof Diva*, 202.

19. The success of multiracial and multiethnic models on the runways and in advertising

images does not, for the most part, extend to acting careers. The film medium tends to be characterized by a more rigid color line separating roles written with racial identity in mind from roles in which race is unspecified. Invariably when race is not specified, a character is white by default.

20. P. David Marshall, *Celebrity and Power: Fame in Contemporary Culture* (Minneapolis: University of Minnesota Press, 1997).

21. Piper, "Passing for White, Passing for Black," 275.

22. Quoted in Joan Morgan, "Free at Last: Mariah Carey," *Essence,* April 2005, 118.

23. James Patrick Herman, "There's Something about Mariah," *Mirabella,* May 1999, 128.

24. Piper, "Passing for White, Passing for Black," 276.

25. Ibid., 277.

26. Alice Walker, "If the Present Looks Like the Past, What Does the Future Look Like?" *In Search of Our Mother's Gardens,* 291.

27. According to gossip circulating when Miguel and Carey were together, Latino talk shows and tabloids labeled her a tramp that brought him down. There are fascinating implications here regarding discourses of purity and contamination that are projected onto Carey, both as a woman of black heritage and as an American. Such a characterization brings to mind Jennifer DeVere Brody's research on the ways that the identity of the gentleman of Victorian England was constructed in reference to the image of the American as feminized and racially impure (*Impossible Purities*).

28. "When Today's Stars Were Almost Famous," *Star,* August 14, 2001, 30.

29. Richard Dyer, "White," *Screen* 29, no. 4 (1988): 44–64.

30. John Berger, *Ways of Seeing* (New York: Penguin, 1990).

31. Patricia J. Williams, "American Kabuki," in *Birth of a Nation'hood: Gaze, Script and Spectacle in the O. J. Simpson Case,* ed. Toni Morrison and Claudia Lacour (New York: Pantheon, 1997), 283–84. Notwithstanding Williams's astute comments, many self-identified black women need not manipulate their hair to conform to white standards of appearance. The Afro of the 1960s and '70s eluded many African Americans who didn't possess a kinky enough hair texture. Kathe Sandler, *A Question of Color,* VHS (1992, San Francisco: Film Two Productions/California Newsreel). In Senna's *Caucasia,* Deck's "Jewfro" indicates that black men also tried and failed to embody the aesthetics of "real" black style.

32. Mariah Carey appeared on the cover of numerous magazines aimed at a primarily white female audience around the turn of the twenty-first century. These included *Mirabella* (May 1999), *Glamour* (November 1999), *Jane* (April 1999) and *Elle* (July 2001). Carey was rarely featured on the cover of black women's magazines until the early 2000s.

33. Kobena Mercer, *Welcome to the Jungle: New Positions in Black Cultural Studies* (New York: Routledge, 1994), 105.

34. Although Carey's hair can be kinkier than in the *Vibe* magazine cover image, even in what the tabloid *Star* called her "bird's nest" stage, it would hardly qualify as

"nappy." By contrast, Keys's hair texture, always styled in cornrows or covered with scarves, remained a mystery. Although some might assume that braids and locks require a certain hair texture, in fact any type of hair can assume any type of style with the right stylist and products. Thus, there was no reason to assume that Keys's hair was particularly kinky until images such as *Vibe*'s cover exposed her "naps."

35. Shaheem Reid, "Eve, Alicia Keys Team Up for Some "Gangsta Love," mtv.com/news, May 22, 2002, accessed March 2, 2009.

36. Diana Jean Schemo, "Despite Options on Census, Many to Check 'Black' Only," *New York Times,* February 12, 2000, A1.

37. Trinh T. Minh-ha, *Woman, Native, Other: Writing Postcoloniality and Feminism* (Bloomington: Indiana University Press, 1989).

38. Mark Anthony Neal, "A Woman's Worth? Alicia Keys Meets Habermas," Popmatters, accessed February 18, 2009, www.popmatters.com/music/videos/k/keys-alicia-woman.shtml.

39. Mariah Carey and Alicia Keys were raised by single mothers. Carey's station in life prior to fame appears to have been closer to the working class. Keys attended Columbia University before receiving her first record contract (she did not earn a degree). At that age Mariah Carey worked at coat check counters in New York nightclubs. Carey did not attend college.

40. Angela Y. Davis, *Are Prisons Obsolete?* (New York: Seven Stories Press, 2003); Ruthie Gilmore, *Golden Gulag: Prisons, Surplus, Crisis, and Opposition in Globalizing California* (Berkeley: University of California Press, 2007).

41. Courtney Marshall, "Law, Literature and the Black Female Subject" (Ph.D. diss., University of California, Los Angeles, 2009); Gina Dent, "Stranger Inside," (Lecture, University of California, Santa Cruz, Spring 2000).

42. Gloria Hull, Patricia Bell, and Barbara Smith, eds., *But Some of Us Are Brave: All the Women Are White, All the Blacks Are Men: Black Women's Studies* (New York: The Feminist Press, 1982).

43. Example of Kemba Smith, granted clemency in 2000 by President Clinton, http://kembasmithfoundation.org/

44. Kanye West, *Gold Digger* (Roc-a-Fella/Def Jam Records, July 2005).

45. Mary J. Blige precedes Alicia Keys as a model for how African American women performers transition between incarnations of femininity and speak across genres, especially with regard to taking men to task for how they mistreat women.

46. Mimi Valdéz, "Blaze of Glory," *Vibe,* March 2004, 126.

47. Prior to 2000 or so, film theorists consistently identified Susan Kohner as "white" when discussing the key difference between the two adaptations of *Imitation of Life*. Following heightened awareness of mixed-race heritage, writers began noting Kohner's parentage: her mother was Mexican film actress Lupita Tovar, her father Jewish-American Paul Kohner. Interestingly, actress Juanita Moore, who played the passing character's mother Annie Mae in 1959, revealed that Susan Kohner was troubled by her character's desire to pass as white. Kohner's identification with her own mixed-race heritage heightened her awareness of the

vexed politics of racial passing. See supplemental materials in *Imitation of Life: Two-Movie Special Edition* (DVD, Universal Studios, 2008).

48. Joan Morgan, "Free at Last," *Essence,* April, 2005, 119. The same issue of *Essence* features two articles by African American women that also articulate struggles linked to the persistence of racial essentialism and notions of racial authenticity. "Will I ever be black enough?" expresses how a woman with two black parents who nevertheless looks "mixed-race" experiences hostility and rejection from African Americans (Kenya Jones, 124). "This child is mine," conveys the frustration of a woman who is often not recognized as the biological mother of her biracial daughter (Lisa Teasley, 106).

49. Lola Ogunnaike, "Through the Fire," *Vibe,* March 2003, 118.

50. Mimi Valdéz, "Blaze of Glory," *Vibe,* March 2004.

51. Naomi Pabst, "Blackness/Mixedness: Contestations Over Crossing Signs," *Cultural Critique* 54 (Spring 2003): 178–212, Aaron C. Allen, "Negotiating Manhood: Exploring Mixed-Race Male Identity's Intersection with Black Masculinity in Gregory Howard Williams's *Life on the Color Line*" (M.A. thesis, University of California, Los Angeles, May 2008).

52. Due to the ups and downs that characterize many artistic careers, Mariah Carey has released more than one album hailed as a "comeback."

5. From Tragedy to Triumph: Dorothy Dandridge, Halle Berry, and the Search for a Black Screen Goddess

1. Richard Dyer, "White," *Screen* 40, no. 1 (1999): 115–19.

2. Mia Mask has argued that the historical trajectory from Dorothy Dandridge to Halle Berry is a matter of a transition from the tragic mulatto, a narrative figure of literature and in Dandridge's case film, to the biracial beauty, with Berry as the example of a celebrity produced by multiculturalism and the emergence of politicized mixed-race identities. See Mask, "Monster's Ball," *Film Quarterly* 58, no. 1 (Fall 2004): 44–55.

3. M. M. Bahktin, *The Dialogic Imagination: Four Essays,* ed. Michael Holquist (Austin: University of Texas Press, 1982).

4. "Dandridge" is the maiden name of the nation's first "first lady" Martha Washington, who brought a significant fortune from her Virginia land-holding family into her marriage with George Washington.

5. Judging from Madame Sul-Te-Wan's photograph and film appearances, rumors about her passing seem at odds with her dark skin; she was not a mulatto/a. However, Hollywood lore maintained that she was Griffith's mistress, and she had small roles in all of his films. See "Mme. Sul-Te-Wan Rites Tomorrow," *Los Angeles Times* Feb. 5, 1959.

6. The Motion Picture Production Code of 1930 (otherwise known as the Hays Code) established a set of guidelines to address the growing influence of popular cinema on the American public. The sixth prohibition in the "Sex" category

was "Miscegenation (sex between the white and black races) is forbidden." See Elaine Walls Reed, "A Very Unusual Practise [*sic*]": Miscegenation and the Film Industry in the Hays Era," West Virginia University, Department of Foreign Languages (July 31, 2005).

7. Donald Bogle, *Dorothy Dandridge: A Biography* (New York: Amistad, 1997), 298.

8. Several years later, the film *Porgy and Bess* went even further in evacuating the erotic potential in a relationship between Dorothy Dandridge as Bess and her leading man, Sidney Poitier; whose character Porgy is paralyzed below the waist.

9. "Why Dandridge Can't Kiss Her White Film Lover," *Jet*, December 1956.

10. "Halle Berry," *Ebony*, August 1999, 90–98.

11. Dorothy Dandridge/Halle Berry, accessed October 1998, www.johnadams.net/cases/samples/Berry-Dandridge/index.html.

12. These actresses include Diana Ross, Cicely Tyson, Diahann Carroll, and Angela Bassett. The nomination of both Ross (*Mahogany*) and Tyson (*Sounder*) in 1972 for the Best Actress award was unprecedented and has not been repeated. Halle Berry did not mention any of these women in her Academy Awards acceptance speech. Nor did she acknowledge Whoopi Goldberg, herself the recipient of a Best Supporting Actress award, who hosted the ceremony in 2002.

13. The late Whitney Houston bought the rights to Donald Bogle's biography of Dandridge. Halle Berry secured rights to the biography written by Earl Mills. One could argue that Jackson and Houston might have played the Dandridge role more convincingly since both are singers and stage performers—artistic pursuits that were important in Dandridge's career and provided her bread and butter when her acting career proved disappointing after *Carmen Jones* (1954). In fact Dandridge's real-life comeback, which was in process when she died, involved cabaret singing rather than a motion picture.

14. Bogle, *Dorothy Dandridge*, 256.

15. For an extended run that Dandridge performed at the Mocambo club in Los Angeles in 1953, impressario Charlie Morrison launched a publicity campaign referencing Alfred Kinsey's recently published *Sexual Behavior of the Human Female*. Advertising copy for the show claimed Dandridge was "a volume of sex with the living impact of the Kinsey report." Ibid., 253.

16. Ibid., 278.

17. Ibid., 450.

18. An ongoing debate among black feminist scholars considers the impact of mulatto/a heroes—and especially heroines—in African American literary history. Were they written to appeal to a white readership likely to sympathize with "virtually white" characters? Some feminist readers have decried early African American novels with representations that draw a clear line between refined, silky-haired, ivory and cream-colored women and their coarser, ugly, dark-skinned sisters. See Alice Walker, "If the Present Looks Like the Past, What Does the Future Look Like?" in *In Search of our Mother's Gardens* (New York: Harcourt Brace Jovanovich, 1983), 290–312. Others have argued for a more nuanced view

of mulatto/a characters as critiques of structural inequalities of race and gender, a perspective that subverts the dichotomy of "positive" and "negative" racial representations. See Barbara T. Christian, *Black Women Novelists: The Development of a Tradition, 1892–1976* (Westport, CT: Greenwood Press, 1980); Hazel V. Carby, *Reconstructing Womanhood* (New York: Oxford University Press, 1987).

19. See Jane Gaines, *Fire and Desire: Mixed-Race Movies in the Silent Era* (Chicago: University of Chicago Press, 2001).

20. Nella Larsen, *Quicksand and Passing;* Julie Dash, *Daughters of the Dust,* VHS (New York: Kino International Corporation, 1992).

21. Harriet Ann Jacobs, *Incidents in the Life of a Slave Girl* (Boston, 1861).

22. Frances Ellen Watkins, *Iola Leroy* (New York: Oxford University Press, 1988); Julie Dash, *Illusions,* VHS (New York: Women Make Movies, 1982)

23. See Monique Guillory, "Under One Roof: The Sins and Sanctities of the New Orleans Quadroon Balls," in *Race Consciousness: African American Studies for the New Century,* ed. Judith Jackson Fossett and Jeffrey A. Tucker (New York: New York University Press, 1997).

24. Berry starred in the short-lived 1980s sitcom *Living Dolls* about fashion models. Berry's first "race-blind" role was as "Rosetta Stone" in *The Flintstones* (dir. Brian Levant, 1994).

25. The number of black cultural figures with iconic status significantly increased in the 1990s: Michael Jordan, Tiger Woods, and Oprah Winfrey are examples. I examined this thread of analysis in chapter 4 (Carey and Keys). All these figures are, however, sports stars and entertainers—actors or musicians. Wanda Coleman has written that America will only allow black criminals and clowns to be successful. Andrea Junot interviewed Coleman for the publication *Angry Women* (Junot Books, 1999).

26. James Baldwin, "*Carmen Jones:* The Light Is Dark Enough," *Notes of a Native Son* in *James Baldwin: Collected Essays* (New York: American Library Collection, 1998), 42.

27. A striking instance of such a moment is photographer Alfred Eisenstaedt's "VJ Day in Times Square," taken August 14, 1945, and subsequently published in *Life* magazine. Although this image is routinely interpreted as joyfully spontaneous, the woman is awkwardly twisted toward the man, who has her head in the vise of his arm, effectively restraining her. If he were to release her suddenly, her lack of balance would surely result in her falling down. The caption in *Life* read, "In New York's Times Square a white-clad girl clutches her purse and skirt as an uninhibited sailor plants his lips squarely on hers."

28. Given Queen Latifah's Oscar-nominated role as "Mama" Morton, the dyke prison warden in the film *Chicago* (2002), the "bitch slap" she delivered to Brody's butt is a clever reference to prison. Latifah is an edgy figure—having played both lesbian and implicitly lesbian characters (*Set It Off,* 1998). Interestingly Queen Latifah also launched a career as a glamorous brand in the early 2000s. She became the spokesmodel for the Curvations line of lingerie for plus-size women when it debuted in 2003. Even more impressively, Latifah is the face for the eponymously named "Queen" collection for Cover Girl cosmetics.

6. High (Mulatto) Hopes: The Rise and Fall of Philippa Schuyler

1. Schuyler was born on August 2, 1931, and died on May 9, 1967. The *Loving vs. State of Virginia* appeal was decided on June 12, 1967.
2. Schuyler's biographer speculates that the only marriage(s) to rival the Schuylers' in terms of media coverage were Jack Johnson's. See Kathryn Talalay, *Composition in Black and White: The Life of Philippa Schuyler* (New York: Oxford University Press, 1995), 12.
3. Ibid., 7.
4. Philippa Schuyler, "My Black and White World," *Sepia*, June 1962, 10–15.
5. "2000 at St. Patrick's attend Requiem for Philippa Schuyler," *New York Times*, May 19, 1967.
6. The content analysis of news media in this chapter includes numerous items from the Philippa Duke Schuyler Collection, Manuscripts, Archives, and Rare Books Division, Schomburg Center for Research in Black Culture; New York Public Library. All materials cited from the collection are noted "SCRBC, NYPL."
7. Black newspapers cited in this chapter include the *Atlanta Daily World*, the *Baltimore African American*, the *Black Dispatch* (Oklahoma City), the *Chicago Defender*, the *Cincinnati Union*, the *New York Amsterdam News*, the *New York Age*, the *Philadelphia Tribune*, the *Pittsburgh Courier*, and the *Washington Tribune*. White newspapers include the *New York Herald Tribune*, the *New York Journal*, the *New York World-Telegram*, the *New York Post*, and the *New York Times*.
8. See Stanley Nelson, dir., *The Black Press: Soldiers without Swords* (San Francisco: California Newsreel, 1998).
9. Schuyler was also featured in intellectually and politically oriented journals such as *The Crisis* (founded by W. E. B. Du Bois in 1912 and still publishing) and *Opportunity*.
10. See transcript, *Soldiers without Swords*. Black intellectuals such as W. E. B. Du Bois and Zora Neale Hurston warned of the ways integration could have deleterious effects on African American institutions. Contemporary studies track the ways integration resulted in, for example, the closing of excellent all-black schools in the South, and greatly diminished opportunities for black filmmakers whose small independent companies could not compete with the Hollywood machine. See Jacqueline Najuma Stewart, *Migrating to the Movies: Cinema and Black Urban Modernity* (Berkeley: University of California Press, 2005).
11. Talalay, *Composition in Black and White*, 224.
12. Nella Larsen, *Quicksand and Passing*, 53, 55.
13. W. E. B. Du Bois, "On the Training of Black Men," *Atlantic Monthly*, September 1902.
14. Talalay, *Composition in Black and White*, 273.
15. Ibid., 17.
16. Prior to his second marriage to Helen Pitts in 1884, Frederick Douglass was involved

with Ottilie Assing, a German woman, for twenty-six years. The relationship with Assing occurred during his first marriage to Anna Douglass. See Maria Diedrich, *Love across Color Lines*. See also Poppy Cannon, *A Gentle Knight*. Many pre- and most post-*Loving* interracial marriages occur in the middle classes. This pattern differs from the trend in the earliest interracial relationships and marriages, beginning in the seventeenth century, among working-class African American men and Irish immigrant women in the northeastern U.S. See *Love across the Color Line*, ed. Helen Lefkowitz Horowitz and Kathy Peiss (Amherst: University of Massachusetts Press, 1996). This book is a rare example of primary source material documenting an example. See also Shirley Taylor Haizlip, *The Sweeter the Juice* (New York: Simon and Schuster, 1994).

17. Ida B. Wells-Barnett, *On Lynchings* (Amherst, NY: Humanity Books, 2002); Sandra Gunning, *Race, Rape, and Lynching: The Red Record of American Literature, 1890–1912* (New York: Oxford University Press, 1996).

18. Thelma Berlack-Boozer, "Interracial Marriage in America Is Workable—Here's Positive Proof," In the Woman's World (column), *New York Amsterdam News*, May 20, 1939 (SCRBC, NYPL).

19. Talalay, *Composition in Black and White*, 42.

20. Scott Minerbrook, *Divided to the Vein: A Journey into Race and Family* (New York: Harcourt Brace, 1996); James McBride, *The Color of Water: A Black Man's Tribute to His White Mother* (New York, Riverhead Books, 1996). Gregory Howard Williams, *Life on the Color Line: The True Story of a White Boy Who Discovered He Was Black* (New York: Dutton, 1995).

21. Hettie Jones, *How I Became Hettie Jones* (New York: Grove Press, 1996).

22. Yelena Khanga with Susan Jacoby, *Soul to Soul: The Story of a Black Russian American Family, 1865–1992* (New York: W. W. Norton, 1992)

23. Hazel V. Carby, *Reconstructing Womanhood;* Barbara T. Christian, *Black Woman Novelists;* Angela Y. Davis, *Women, Race, and Class;* Paula Giddings, *When and Where I Enter,* and Deborah Gray White, *Ar'n't I a Woman?*

24. See Hortense Spillers, "Mama's Baby, Papa's Maybe: An American Grammar Book," *Black, White, and in Color.*

25. Eva Saks, "Miscegenation Law," in *Interracialism*, ed. Sollors, 61–80.

26. Paul R. Spickard, *Mixed Blood*, 278.

27. Social scientists identify intermarriage as the final stage of assimilating to American national identity. See Stephen Steinberg, *The Ethnic Myth: Race, Ethnicity, and Class in America* (Boston: Beacon Press, 1989).

28. Thelma Berlack-Boozer, "House of Schuyler Centers on Philippa: Genius Desires to be Pianist-Composer Rather than Follow in Parents' Footsteps," In the Woman's World, *New York Amsterdam News*, August 1938 (SCRBC, NYPL).

29. Thelma Berlack-Boozer, "Interracial Marriage in America Is Workable—Here's Positive Proof," In the Woman's World, *New York Amsterdam News*, May 20, 1939 (SCRBC, NYPL).

30. John Langston Gwaltney, *Drylongso;* Dorothy West, *The Wedding.*

31. Gwaltney, *Drylongso.*

32. Ibid.

33. Gloria Wade-Gayles, "A Change of Heart about Matters of the Heart: An Anger Shift from Interracial Marriages to Real Problems," in *Rooted Against the Wind: Personal Essays* (Boston: Beacon Press, 1996), 93. Wade-Gayles cites W. E. B. Du Bois, *The Souls of Black Folk* (A. C. McClurg, 1904).

34. Eva Saks, "Representing Miscegenation Law," in *Interracialism,* ed. Sollors.

35. United States Supreme Court, *Loving v. Virginia,* 388 United States 1. Appeal from the Supreme Court of Appeals of Virginia. No. 395. http://laws.findlaw.com/us/388/1.html. Accessed August 1, 2008.

36. "George Schuylers have a baby girl," *Baltimore African American,* August 5, 1931, front page. "It's a girl!" *New York Amsterdam News,* August 5, 1931 (SCRBC, NYPL).

37. Joseph W. Alsop Jr., "Harlem's Youngest Philosopher Parades Talent on 3rd Birthday," *New York Herald Tribune,* August 3, 1934 (SCRBC, NYPL).

38. Nora Holt, "Philipa [*sic*], Musical Prodigy, Seems to Improve with Age." *New York Amsterdam News,* August 12, 1944 (SCRBC, NYPL).

39. Maye Opitz and Katherine Oguntoye, eds., *Showing Our Colors: Afro-German Women Speak Out* (Amherst: University of Massachusetts Press, 1992); Rebekah Walker, *Black, White, and Jewish: Autobiography of a Shifting Self* (New York: Riverhead Books, 2001).

40. Edwin Black, *War against the Weak: Eugenics and America's Campaign to Create a Master Race* (New York: Thunder's Mouth Press, 2003).

41. Ibid.

42. Joel Williamson, *New People: Miscegenation and Mulattoes in the United States* (Baton Rouge: Louisiana State University Press, 1995); F. James Davis, *Who Is Black? One Nation's Definition;* Eva Saks, "Miscegenation Law."

43. "500 Young Pianists in Rating Contest: Negro Girl, 6, Adds Composition of Her Own to Repertoire Works by Masters," *Cincinnati Union,* June 16, 1938; "Harlem Girl, 6, Wins Medal as Pianist in City Contest: Philippa Schuyler, Composer of 30 Pieces, Honored in Finals on Mall," *New York Post,* June 20, 1938; "Harlem Prodigy 6 Today, Turns More Musical: Own and Classical Works Now Accorded Place in Repertoire of Negro Girl," *New York Herald Tribune,* August 2, 1937, all SCRBC, NYPL.

44. "What Happens to Negro Child Geniuses," *Jet,* December 11, 1952 (44–48); "Uncle Sam's Top Genius: Prodigy of a Black and White Marriage Whose Mentality Baffles Science," *Color,* December 1952 (SCRBC, NYPL).

45. Similarly The *New York Amsterdam News* birth announcement reads: "It's a girl! Mr. and Mrs. George S. Schuyler welcomed . . . [t]heir baby, who in time may be a columnist and novelist . . ." (SCRBC, NYPL).

46. "A Pianist-Poet Reaches 6 and Still She's No Prodigy: Harlem Parents Credit Intellectual Attainments of Child to Training and Diet, as Usual—But You Should Hear Girl Spell and Play," *New York Herald Tribune,* August 2, 1937 (SCRBC, NYPL).

47. Bernice Dutrielle, "Philippa Schuyler, Youthful Prodigy, Sets Ole Quakertown on Its Musical Ear at Recital," *Philadelphia Tribune,* March 2, 1939 (SCRBC, NYPL).

48. Charles Neville, "The Curse of Genius," Fall 1938 (no publication indicated) (SCRBC, NYPL).

49. "Philippa Schuyler Charms Here in Artistic Recital," *Pittsburgh Courier,* December 3, 1938; "Brooklyn Y.W.C.A. Gives 11th Holiday Morning Muscle," *New York Age,* March 5, 1938; "Big Audience Hears Child Musician," *Boston Guardian,* January 29, 1939. "Philippa Is Given Gold Medal by Music League," *The Pittsburgh Courier,* June 17, 1939 (SCRBC, NYPL).

50. See P. David Marshall, *Celebrity and Power: Fame in Contemporary Culture,* (Minneapolis: University of Minnesota Press, 1997).

51. "Philippa's Day at the Fair," *Time,* July 1, 1940 (SCRBC, NYPL).

52. "The Shirley Temple of America's Negroes," *Look,* January 1, 1939 (SCRBC, NYPL).

53. Edythe Robertson, "Music Education League Awards Presented at Radio City Theatre" (no newspaper noted, no date, most likely 1938) (SCRBC, NYPL).

54. Concert Program, *The Crisis,* April 1938 (SCRBC, NYPL).

55. Talalay, *Composition in Black and White,* 79.

56. "Women of Today Get Medallions," *New York Amsterdam News,* July 1, 1939 (SCRBC, NYPL).

57. "Black Is Honored for Aid to Negro," *New York Times,* February 10, 1941; Press release, "The Honor Roll in Race Relations for 1940" (SCRBC, NYPL).

58. "Harlem Girl, 6, Wins Medal as Pianist in City Contest: Philippa Schuyler, Composer of 30 Pieces, Honored in Finals on Mall," *New York Post,* June 20, 1938 (SCRBC, NYPL).

59. "Harlem Prodigy," *Time,* June 22, 1936; "Philippa's Day at the Fair," *Time,* July 1, 1940; Joseph Mitchell, "Reporter at Large: An Evening with a Gifted Child," *New Yorker,* August 31, 1940 (all SCRBC, NYPL).

60. "Philippa Schuyler Charms Here in Artistic Recital," *Pittsburgh Courier,* December 3, 1938 (SCRBC, NYPL).

61. Thelma Berlack-Boozer, "Interracial Marriage in America Is Workable—Here's Positive Proof," *New York Amsterdam News,* In the Woman's World, May 20, 1939 (SCRBC, NYPL).

62. Bernice Dutrielle, "Philippa Schuyler, Youthful Prodigy, Sets Ole Quakertown on Its Musical Ear at Recital," *Philadelphia Tribune,* March 2, 1939 (SCRBC, NYPL).

63. "Big Audience Hears Child Musician," *Boston Guardian,* January 29, 1939 (SCRBC, NYPL).

64. Beatrice Adair, "Harlem's Child Prodigy," *Silhouette* (Los Angeles Pictorial Magazine), April 1939 (SCRBC, NYPL).

65. "Musical Genius Is Six Years Old," *Washington Tribune,* August 7, 1937 (SCRBC, NYPL).

66. "Philippa's Six: Celebrates Natal Day in Parisian Dress," *New York Amsterdam News,* August 7, 1937; "Philippa Is Given Gold Medal by Music League," *Pittsburgh Courier,* June 17, 1939; "Cuba Loves Phillipa [*sic*]," Music Notes, *New York Amsterdam News,* September 27, 1952 (all SCRBC, NYPL).

67. "Meet the George Schuylers, America's Strangest Family," *Our World,* April 1951 (23–26) (SCRBC, NYPL).

68. "One Last Look Around in 1949: Beautiful Genius," *Pittsburgh Courier,* December 31, 1949.

"At seventeen takes her place among our most beautiful women." *Atlanta Daily World,* 1950 (SCRBC, NYPL). (In 1950 Schuyler turned nineteen.)

69. Alton Adams, "Philippa Duke Schuyler: A Paradoxical Genius," *Photo News* (St. Thomas Virgin Islands), February 15, 1950 (SCRBC, NYPL).

70. Charlotte Amalie, "Capacity Audience Hails Pianist" *Photo News,* March 15, 1950 (SCRBC, NYPL).

71. Kitty Kingston, "Philippa Schuyler—the incredible," *Daily Gleaner* (Kingston, Jamaica), April 1952 (SCRBC, NYPL).

72. Ibid.

73. Felipe Elosegui, "1000 Noticias en Sepia," *Excelsior* (Havana, Cuba), May 1952 (SCRBC, NYPL).

74. "Cuba Loves Phillipa: Poetry Joins Music for Delightful Eve," Music Notes, *New York Amsterdam News,* September 27, 1952 (SCRBC, NYPL).

75. Philippa Schuyler, "Why I Don't Marry," *Ebony,* July 1958 (78–84); "A Pianist Tours the Congo," *Hue* 6, no. 7 (May 1959): 56–59; "She's Been There," Review of "My Adventures in Black and White," *Sepia,* March 1961; Philippa Schuyler, "My Black and White World," *Sepia,* June 1962 (10–15) (SCRBC, NYPL).

76. "Europe's Elite Heard America's Music Envoy," *Color (News O' The World),* April 1954 (39); "Notables Hear Pianist Speak on African Tour," *New York Age,* April 26, 1958; "A Pianist Tours the Congo," *Hue* 6, no. 7 (May 1959): 56–59 (SCRBC, NYPL).

77. Nora Holt, "Sylvia Olden-Lee, Concert Pianist," (Music) *New York Amsterdam News,* July 29, 1944 (SCRBC, NYPL).

78. Talalay, *Composition in Black and White,* 129, 145, 183 (SCRBC, NYPL).

79. "NBC Grooms a New Piano Star (Natalie Hinderas)," *Jet,* November 5, 1953, 60–61 (SCRBC, NYPL).

80. "Europe's Elite Heard America's Music Envoy," *Color,* April 1954 (SCRBC, NYPL).

81. "Philippa Schuyler Makes Debut at Town Hall," *Jet,* May 28, 1953, 59 (SCRBC, NYPL).

82. French critic's review of Felipa Monterro debut at Kammermusikaal April 30, 1963 (Zurich, Switzerland), May 8, 1963 (SCRBC, NYPL).

83. Philippa Schuyler, "My Black and White World," *Sepia,* June 1962, 13 (SCRBC, NYPL).

84. James Baldwin, "The Discovery of What It Means to Be an American," *Ideas Across Time: Classic and Contemporary Readings for Composition,* ed. Igor Webb (New York: McGraw-Hill, 2008), 29–35.

85. *Felipa Monterro* clippings file, 1960–1965. Schuyler corresponded with Reverend Uriah Fields as Monterro in 1964 (SCRBC, NYPL).

86. Kerry Ann Rocquemore and David L. Brunsma, *Beyond Black;* Kathleen Odell Korgen, *From Black to Biracial;* Kimberly McClain Da Costa, *Making Multiracials;* Kim M. Williams, *Mark One or More: Civil Rights in Multiracial America;* Lise Funderberg, *Black, White, Other.*

INDEX

Adams, Alton, 120

Affleck, Ben, 64

African American elite, 36, 80, 135n4, 137n24; and skin color, 26, 33; strategic marriage practiced by, 26, 110; *The Wedding* portrayal of, 23–24, 29, 35

African American History Month, 24, 29, 38

African Americans, 45, 97, 135n4, 138n4; adoption of one-drop rule by, 32, 35, 57, 91; and biracial identity, 15–16, 35, 38, 45–46, 54–55, 57–58, 75; color hierarchies among, 36; identification of blackness by, 55, 137–38n34; Native American heritage among, 42; policing of racial boundaries by, 35–36, 71; on racial authenticity, 71, 80

African American women, 6, 41–42, 73, 78; and beauty, 30, 71; as entertainers, 87, 143n45; femininity of, 81, 93; in Hollywood, 88, 93, 98; and intermarriage, 6–7; sexuality of, 5, 94, 97, 100, 109; and skin color, 82, 97; vulnerability to coerced sex, 31, 109. *See also* black/white women

Afro-centrism, 10, 39, 41, 81

Afro hair style, 42, 142n31

Albert of Monaco, Prince, 22

Alsop, Joseph, 114

Anderson, Eddie, 116

Arsenio Hall Show, 66

assimilation, 110, 148n27

Badu, Erykah, 68, 73

Bailey, Pearl, 95

Baldwin, James, 98, 125

Baltimore African American, 104

Bamboozled (Lee), 136n5

Bassett, Angela, 145n12

Beavers, Louise, 93

Belafonte, Harry, 90

Benét, Eric, 102

Berger, John, 73

Bernhard, Sandra, 69–70

Berry, Halle, 12, 72; awards for, 89, 91, 98; biracial heritage of, 90–91, 94, 96, 102–3; career of, 91, 96, 101; in *Catwoman*, 64–65; and Dandridge, 11, 89, 91–93, 96–98, 101; as icon of beauty, 62, 91, 94, 144n2; in *Monster's Ball*, 89–90, 98–101; personal life of, 101–2; television roles of, 98, 137n29; in *The Wedding*, 23, 30, 33–34, 36, 38, 98

CAROLINE A. STREETER is an associate professor in the Department of English and the Ralph J. Bunche Center for African American Studies at the University of California, Los Angeles. She was the first undergraduate student to earn a B.A. in Feminist Studies at Stanford University. In the Ph.D. program in Ethnic Studies at the University of California, Berkeley, she was in the vanguard of scholars creating contemporary mixed-race studies in the United States. Streeter was born in Alsace, France, and grew up living in France, Germany, Colorado, California, New York, Austria, and Saudi Arabia. She has become a long-term California transplant, living and thriving in Los Angeles.